Dancing in the Rain

Dancing
in the Rain

*a memoir of courage,
strength, and resilience*

NELLA COIRO

Library of Congress Control Number: 2022937278
ISBN (paperback) 978-1-7339522-3-1
ISBN (e-book): 978-1-7339522-4-8

Published in the United States by:
Sunrise Valley Publishers
New York

Author's website: nellacoiro.com
Interior book design & book cover: Ariel Hudnall

DISCLAIMER
This book references actual events in the life of the author as truthfully
as recollection permits. While all persons within are actual individuals,
names and identifying characteristics have been changed to respect
their privacy.

Dedication

This book is dedicated to my husband, Kenny.
Thank you for your support, insights, for patiently listening
to endless revisions of this book, and for being such a
loving life partner throughout the years.

In Loving Memory

*In loving memory of my basset hound Penelope,
who had a big personality, and helped to mold, teach,
and change me in significant ways. She earned her angel
wings during the writing of this book. Run free, my sweet
baby girl, until we meet again in heaven.*

9/24/2009 – 9/10/2020

Contents

Acknowledgements

**I want to thank and acknowledge the
following special individuals:**

To Dr. Lynne Hoffman: Thank you for walking with me through a lifetime of journeys and adversity, with caring, compassion, confrontation when necessary, understanding, and unyielding support. You have taught me so much about relationships and life. Last but not least, thanks for reading the chapters of this book piecemeal, and offering your feedback.

To Dr. Michael Capicotto: When we began my dialysis journey, you said, "We're in this together," and have consistently kept your word! You are kind-hearted, smart, understanding, and, in all ways, you personify the word "healer."

To my dear friend, Nicole Russell, for helping my heart to heal when I lost my Penelope, and my heart was shattered to pieces.

To the nurses and the technicians at the DaVita Dialysis Center, for your hard work, for keeping me alive, for your warmth, your smiles, your compassion, pep talks, and interesting conversation.

A special shout-out to my renal social worker, Nicole Stratton. You are a burst of sunshine! Thank you for your kindness and empathy, and for having a great sense of humor. I appreciate the times when you've brought a smile to my face when I had tears in my eyes.

Special thanks to my editor, Audrey Silverman. Thank you for the extraordinary work you've done on all of my books, and for your input, insights, and guidance. You have helped me to grow, and to become a better writer. It's been a pleasure to work with you.

Foreword

I HAVE KNOWN AND WORKED WITH NELLA for almost 30 years. I have been at her side as she has sought to understand, and triumph over the many traumas, large and small, that largely defined her childhood, and, to a significant degree, her adult life. The journey has been arduous, but ultimately, largely successful. Nella is very different now than the woman I met three decades ago.

When asked to describe Nella, the two words that come to mind are resilient and courageous. It takes strength to withstand an upbringing punctuated by abuse and neglect, and emerge with one's sense of humanity intact. It takes courage to be emotionally available to others, knowing full well how vulnerable caring for someone renders you. And finally, it takes enormous courage (and generosity) to revisit your past, reprocess it's events, and produce a memoir, with the hope that it will help someone else to heal.

As one goes through this book, I hope Nella's story will inspire those that need to face their own demons, and triumph over their own versions of adversity. Her journey proves it can be done.

—Dr. Lynne Hoffman

Preface

'VE DREAMED ABOUT WRITING BOOKS my entire life, but I was a procrastinator, and lacked the self-discipline and motivation to do so. In 2019, my doctor told me my kidneys were failing and I needed to be put on dialysis. This life-changing moment was a wake-up call, and motivated me to fulfill this dream.

Consequently, I wrote two self-help books which were well received, and they've helped a lot of people. However, this memoir is quite different. It's tell-all, at times, gut-wrenching, and deeply personal. I believe that it's also inspiring.

Since much of the adversity, emotional injuries, and pain inflicted upon me involved immediate family members, it hasn't been easy to be objective. However, to the best of my ability, I've tried to focus on the facts, and to write this memoir fairly, truthfully, and without malice.

As I wrote this memoir, I had to re-live some of the most upsetting and heartbreaking moments in my life. There were times when I continued to write, even as I've actively cried, and other times, when I had to stop writing, and take a walk to compose myself, and clear my head.

As I continued to write, and push beyond my comfort zone, I was able look beyond some of my painful past experiences, and recognize the resilience, courage, and hope that resonated throughout my story. Furthermore, I was able to identify the insights I had gained and the lessons I had learned, even in the worst of circumstances.

Some of the stories in this memoir have never been shared before. I've never had the courage to revisit them or articulate them, because it was so difficult to attach words to these intense memories, never mind saying these words out loud.

Despite the difficulties, I wrote this memoir because I have a story that needs to be told. In the telling, I'm hoping that I can touch someone's life – maybe your life. My goal is to help my reader to make sense of their own life, and to know that they're not alone, and they too can rise above the adversity that they might find themselves in.

I have paraphrased some of the dialogue, because it was impossible to remember the exact words in each conversation. To protect the privacy of the individuals mentioned in this book, I've used pseudonyms, and changed some of the identifying characteristics. However, I realize that there are still some people who might be disturbed that I revealed *family secrets*, and I accept this possibility.

Chapter 1
Beginnings

MY BEGINNINGS MUST HAVE BEEN INTENSE. I imagine that the time spent in the womb of my frightened, seventeen-year-old birth mother, Theresa, might have been overshadowed by feelings of shame, fear, sadness, and conflict, as she carried me to term, knowing that she was being pressured to give me away.

Then, I was adopted by Jimmy and Maria, who were married for ten years, unable to conceive, and desperately wanted children. Perhaps they appeared to be a nice couple. They might have even began with good intentions, and a desire to be good parents. And yet... from my perspective... they weren't. They had a lot of unresolved issues and unhealed wounds that fed into their parenting. Maria, the only mother I've ever known, projected a formidable and frightening presence, and, in some ways, remnants of this oppressive energy still linger.

Although I found it difficult and challenging to rise above my history, I have always been determined not allow my beginnings to dictate the trajectory of my entire life.

To a great extent, and with much work, I've risen about my circumstances. Although I've struggled, I've achieved many of my life goals.

Ironically, some of my early experiences have helped me to cultivate the strength and resilience I've needed to overcome other obstacles that I've encountered throughout my life. In a roundabout way, every negative experience have prepared me to face future challenges.

Then, there are the complexities of nature versus nurture. Although there's an adage, *blood is thicker than water*, I believe that history is much thicker than blood. Although I'm not blood-related to my family, there's a history, and it's powerful – far more powerful than DNA. For better or for worse, this history has contributed to the woman that I am today. In a sense, I've inherited, and needed to heal from a dysfunctional mentality, even if it didn't come from my genes.

Although it was easy to remove myself from the toxic environment I grew up in, it has taken a lot of work and determined effort to extract the dysfunction from within me. It's been difficult to shed old versions of myself, while trying to embrace new ways of relating to the world, and interacting with others, without fear and guarded defensiveness. There were times when I've taken a few steps backwards, before moving forward once again.

As strange as this might sound, although I've been damaged by the physical traumas of my past, I've been far more damaged by my mother's consistent and unrelenting psychological abuse, and some of this pain still remains. However, if I look at my life in its entirety, I can see that the strength I've accrued from my struggles has prepared me to address and handle other adversity.

Chapter 2
Indelible Reflections

A S I REFLECT UPON MY CHILDHOOD YEARS, nearly every memory indicates that my parents were was severely dysfunctional. Many of these memories are tattooed in my mind with indelible ink. Regardless of how hard I try, I simply cannot erase them from my thoughts and my heart. I cannot remember a single time – a birthday, a holiday, or any potentially happy event, that didn't end with discord.

No one spoke in a normal tone of voice, especially my mother. There was constant tension, yelling and arguing. Echoes of "Goddamnit!" – "Stop it!" – "You're driving me crazy!" – "Leave me alone!" routinely reverberated throughout the house.

My mother didn't have a warm, nurturing personality. She didn't hug, or offer words of love, encouragement or praise. She certainly wasn't the kind of mom I saw on TV family shows like *The Brady Bunch* or *Leave it to Beaver*.

If someone was doing her a favor, but was unable to complete the task to her satisfaction, instead of being appreciative, she became angry. I remember that once a friend was adding a lock to her door. At the beginning, she would say, "Joe's such a nice guy. He's doing my lock for me." Then, when Joe was unable to install it to her satisfaction, her praise turned into harsh criticism: "What a stupid ass. He can't fix a simple lock?" That's how fast she would switch her opinion of someone.

Since she was argumentative, my other family members usually appeased her, or tried to avoid her. My mother disliked my Aunt Teri the most, and often provoked arguments with her, complaining about her constantly, "I can't stand my sister!"

Usually, my Aunt Teri tried to avoid or ignore my mother. However, there were times when my aunt fought back. On one occasion, she retorted, "Vinni, why do you always want to start trouble for no reason? I just don't understand you. You always want to create problems when there aren't any."

Since my mother wasn't accustomed to being confronted, my aunt's comments upset and offended her. She never considered that she provoked the situation, and was at fault for the conflicts. Instead, she wanted sympathy, "I can't believe my sister said that to me. She hurt my feelings."

My mother also gossiped about her brother Sal, and his wife, Dorothy, rudely commenting: "Can you believe this? Every year he buys her new furniture. His wife must be sitting on gold." Or, "My brother is such an ass." My Aunt Rita was exempt from arguments or criticism, because she enabled and pacified my mother.

My mother lacked finesse or appreciation for others, and could be childish and selfish. This was most evident during the holidays. More often than not, she was unhappy with the gifts she received. Rather than graciously accepting them, as most people do, she would make rude comments, without considering that she might be offending the gift giver; "Why'd you buy me this? I really don't need this," was a common response from her.

After I was married, the holidays became a problem for my mother, because of how my husband and I chose to alternate them. One year we'd spend a particular holiday with her; the next year, we'd spend that holiday with my in-laws. We thought this was fair. She didn't. She wanted us to visit both families on the same day, so she wouldn't "get cheated out of a holiday." We didn't want to do this, because our families didn't live near one another, and doing so would have been extremely inconvenient and stressful.

Several weeks before each holiday, she'd begin her phone calls, saying, "I don't understand why you can't see the both of us."(I should mention that my sister and her husband were spending all of the holidays with her, because they went to both families on the same day. She never had to spend a holiday alone.)

Again and again, I'd explain why we were doing this, and she'd argue with me. "I'm very unhappy with the way you're doing this. Your sister doesn't do it this way." She would spend weeks campaigning for us to join her for all of the holidays. By the time the holiday arrived, I was beyond stressed.

While my mother has always been combative and difficult, my father was the complete opposite. He had a warm and charming personality, a great sense of humor, and a lot of friends. Anyone who met my father immediately liked him. Unlike my mother, my father didn't like arguing, and would do anything to avoid it. However, he too had his demons, and he was also deeply envious, mostly toward other family members.

Since I was rebellious and outspoken, I was dubbed "the problem child," and became the family scapegoat. In contrast, my sister Stella was compliant, and never disagreed with our parents. In some ways, she was the very image of a perfect daughter, especially since she physically resembled my mother. However, my parents also put a lot of pressure on her, and they didn't trust her, so she couldn't be a happy, carefree child either.

In many ways, my sister gradually assumed the maternal role in the family. I'd often hear, "Stella, can you tidy up the house and clean the bathroom? Mommy doesn't feel good today." (Mommy usually didn't *feel good* when it was time to cook, or clean the house.) When we were older, my sister did most of the cooking, and she never complained, while my mother often chain-smoked, and delegated the household chores to her. Rather than being angry at my mother, my sister redirected her anger toward me, because I didn't assist her in doing these chores. (She never let go of this childhood resentment.)

Despite the pressure imposed upon her, Stella has been unable to recognize the origins of her own dysfunction. If asked, she'll tell you that she had a perfect childhood, raised by hard-working parents, who gave her a good life. Since she can't trace her current difficulties back to our toxic childhood, it appears that she has robbed herself of the opportunity to heal, and, more importantly, to stop the cycle from being passed on to her own children.

To be fair, I agree that both of my parents worked hard and had incredibly stressful lives. They provided us with a home, food, a parochial school education, and all of our medical needs. We had birthday parties and holiday celebrations. However, this was overshadowed by the tension-filled, dysfunctional atmosphere, and doesn't erase or justify the toxicity, the abuse, and the lingering pain that it has created.

It's interesting, because during the ten years that my mother was childless, she told other family members that she desperately wanted to be a mother. Then, when she became a mom, she behaved as if she didn't want children, often expressing her discontent: "I'm sorry I had you kids. You're driving me crazy." Or, "You're always aggravating me. I was better off before." Or, simply, "I can't stand you!" I can still remember how frightened and upset I felt when I heard these comments.

I've never heard her say, even once, that she was happy to be a mother, or that she loved us. Perhaps she liked the idea of being a mom, but didn't like the work that it actually entailed. Maybe she thought that children could fix what appeared to be an unhappy marriage, or her dysphoria. Regardless of the reason, her comments made us feel unwanted.

It seemed that my parents were never happy, especially with each other. They argued constantly. I don't know all of the reasons why they were so miserable with one another. However, I do know that, unlike my mother, my father didn't hold a grudge. On the other hand, my mother couldn't forgive or let go of her resentments.

In those days, she refused to accept his apology, saying "Leave me alone. I don't forgive you, Jimmy." When he attempted to hug her, she would push him away. Sometimes she would swing at him, saying, "Get away from me." She would punch him with incredible force, sometimes knocking him off balance. He never hit her back, but sometimes he would react to her physical violence by crying. It was a deeply traumatizing exchange to witness as a child.

I don't remember ever seeing my mother show even a speck of warmth or love toward my father. Sometimes I wondered if she ever had. From my perspective, it seemed that she merely tolerated him at best, and at times, hated him. It appeared that he cared about her, and he was hurt when she rejected or berated him.

And yet, although they both seemed unhappy with each other, divorce was never discussed in those days, because it was taboo. Catholics didn't get divorced, and Italians looked upon a divorced woman as a *puttana*, a woman with low morals. Besides, my mother couldn't support herself.

My mother didn't accept apologies from anyone. Instead, she would become hell-bent on getting revenge, and ponder ways to retaliate. She would tell my sister and I, "Don't get mad, get even. Bide your time, but get even."

She also never apologized to anyone. Since she believed that she was never wrong, and was always the victim, she felt that she had no reason to be apologetic. Even after times when she and I were estranged, and then we reconciled, she never apologized. Rather, her defense was: "I did the best that I could."

The only thing that seemed to make my mother happy was having her hair done, and then, after my father died, she went to local dances for middle-aged folk. However, she seemed to enjoy the disruption she thought she was creating, rather than the dancing. She would return from the dances, excited to tell us stories that rarely seemed credible.

"All the men wanted to dance with me. I think the other women are jealous of me, because they're afraid I'm gonna steal their husbands," she would say. There wasn't much that brought a smile to my mother's face, but the idea that she was disrupting the love lives of other women seemed to do so.

I have often wondered why my mother was so unhappy. In the chapter, *Old Photographs*, I explore photos which showed how her moods seemed to radically shift after she was married. Did an unhappy marriage change her, or was she always that way? I don't know.

However, I do know that my mother's personality remained this way after my father's death, so I don't see how this could've been solely related to their marriage. Nine years later, when my mother remarried, she continued to verbally and physically abuse her second husband, Joe, and continued her psychological abuse with everyone around her, until the day she died, and beyond.

Chapter 3
My Mother's Voice

"CAN YOU TELL THE MORTICIAN to put more red lipstick on your mother?" This was my aunt Teri's request, at my mother's wake and viewing. Although it sounded strange, out of respect, I did as she asked. I guess this brought her some comfort. My mother was the first sibling to die, and this must have been upsetting to my aunts and my uncle.

It was early in the afternoon, and the first viewing, following my mother's death. There were close to a hundred empty chairs, in a large, dimly lit, wood-paneled room. The only people present were my husband Kenny and I, my sister Stella and her husband Rob, and my aunts Teri and Rita. More family members were expected to come during the evening session.

The room was uncomfortably silent, and there was an overwhelming aroma emitting from the floral arrangements placed near the casket. To this day, I can't stand the smell of flowers, because they bring me right back to this moment in time. My brain still equates that smell with death.

I wonder who invented the *wake*, especially the *viewing*. It's a bizarre ritual, and it seems so disrespectful. The deceased is *laid out* in an open casket, and overly dressed – men wearing suits, and women dressed in gowns. The mortician looks at a photograph to prepare the deceased, applying makeup and fixing the hair, attempting to make the person resemble what they looked like when they were alive. But they never really do.

My father was a baker, so he rarely dressed up. He owned one blue iridescent suit that he only wore on special occasions, like weddings or funerals. He was buried in this suit. It was strange to see him lying in a casket in a suit and a tie, when, while he lived, he always dressed casually.

My mother didn't have fancy clothes either. She usually wore casual-type floral dresses, called house-dresses, so we had to purchase her last dress from the funeral director, at a hefty price. It was a beautiful sky-blue gown. My sister liked this dress because, as she said, "It matches mom's blue eyes."

If you've ever been to a wake, then you know how awkward and bizarre the conversations can be. A typical comment is: "She looks so good." I've always thought to myself, *"Seriously? If she looked good, she would be alive."* Then there are others who want to know every single detail that led to the person's death. They're completely insensitive to the fact that when you lose a loved one, this is the last story you want to repeat over and over again. Maybe they just feel uncomfortable, and don't know what to say.

"She looks so peaceful," my Aunt Rita said to no one in particular. I thought about her comment, and glanced toward the casket, taking a closer look at my mother. For the first time I could remember, she didn't look angry or upset. I thought, as strange as it sounded... my mother *did* look peaceful. Maybe her restless spirit had left her body.

Then my Aunt Teri made a comment, and as peculiar as it sounded, it was sad and true: "You know, it's sad that your mother struggled to lose weight her whole life. She had to suffer in the hospital and die, to be thin. I haven't seen her this thin in years."

There was also an event which was rather unusual, and worth mentioning. During the afternoon viewing, my Aunt Teri felt disturbed because there weren't a lot of mourners, so she called all of her friends at her social club, and asked them to attend the wake. None of them knew my mother personally.

One minute, there were six of us sitting in the room, and the next, there were swarms of seniors. I'm guessing that between 50 to 70 people were lined up. It looked like people were on a bus trip, got lost, and accidentally walked into a funeral home. It was bizarre. My sister Stella turned to me and whispered, "Who are all of these people?"

I responded, "I think they're Aunt Teri's friends. Weird, isn't it?" She nodded in agreement.

One by one, each person went up to the casket, kneeled, made the sign of the cross, said a silent prayer, and then came over to my sister and I, and expressed their condolences for a woman that they've never met. My sister and I looked at each other, thinking, *"What the hell?"*

My mother's only lifelong friend, Ann, came to visit her in the hospital once, but didn't come to the wake. The only non-family members at my mother's wake were some of her former coworkers, who came pay their respects during the evening viewings.

Several attendees talked about how my mother suffered before she passed, and how she was brave in the face of other chronic illnesses. I agree that she was quite courageous and resilient against all odds. Other than that, I don't remember conversations recalling any fond memories.

None of this mattered to me. I didn't care about how many people were at my mother's wake, their conversations, or how much red lipstick she needed to improve her appearance. My thoughts drifted elsewhere...

As I sat there, a revelation hit me like a lightning bolt. I suddenly realized that I would never hear my mother's voice again. The voice that annoyed me. The voice that criticized me.

The voice that started unnecessary arguments. The voice that would rather keep quiet, than offer a compliment or a few kind words of approval. The voice that always sounded angry and unhappy. The voice that never said, "I love you."

We didn't have much in common, except for the fact that we were constantly disappointed in one another, and had to learn how to protect ourselves from one another. She wasn't really interested in my life, and I wasn't really interested in hers. And yet, the enormous influence she had over me transcended her death.

It's strange. There were so many times when I wanted to hear my mother's silence, rather than her disapproval, and now... she was silenced forever... And the strangest thing of all is, sometimes I still miss hearing her voice...

Chapter 4
A Basketful of Feelings

"Death ends a life, but it does not end a relationship, which struggles on in the survivor's mind toward some final resolution, which it perhaps never finds." (Robert Anderson)

MY MOTHER WAS BURIED ON A CLOUDY, dismal, autumn morning. Although her casket was lowered into the ground, her memory, and the pain that she caused, weren't buried along with her. Decades later, she is still alive in my thoughts, as I reflect upon the basketful of feelings – the aftermath – that she left me with.

Despite our fractured relationship, my mother had one quality that I admired. She was probably the most courageous woman that I have ever known. Later in life, she developed a slew of medical problems, but giving up was never an option that she ever considered. She was a fighter, and, in many ways, her stubbornness helped her to survive.

"We have to give ourselves courage. No one can do it for us." My mother often said these words, when asked how she dealt with all of her medical problems. And although we didn't agree on much, I share this philosophy. It's bizarre that the quality I hated most about her – her unyielding stubbornness – was also the quality that I most admired.

My mother never backed down from a fight. Never. I was told that even in the final moments of her life, she was fighting to stay alive. "Flailing her arms," were the exact words used by the nurse who was with her. That's powerful. You have to applaud that. She left the world with the same fiery aggression, and unyielding, unapologetic tenacity that she projected during her 73 years on this earth.

Sometimes I think about the seven weeks that she was in the hospital. It began on August 7th, with a phone call from my cousin Joanna: "Your mother is very ill. She can't speak. We're at her house. The ambulance is here, and they're taking her to the hospital now." I was stunned. I felt like I had been hit with a bucket of ice water. I never even considered that I would ever receive a phone call like this. I jotted down the name of the hospital and directions, got into my car, and headed there.

She was still in the E.R. when I arrived, and I burst into tears. I remembered our last phone conversation, and I was overwhelmed with guilt. I began to ramble; I don't remember exactly what I said to her. But I do recall saying, "I've always loved you." I think that I never truly realized that a part of me really did love her until that moment. The problem has always been my belief that it was *she* that never loved me.

My mother had a cerebral hemorrhage, and needed emergency brain stem surgery. Being the warrior that she was, she survived the surgery against the terrible odds. Even her doctors were baffled. Even so, she would never again be able to breathe on her own. In many ways, surviving surgery ended up more of a curse more than a blessing.

It was heartbreaking to see her helpless, lingering, trying to hang on to life by a thread. She was on a respirator, and had lost the ability to speak or write, but I do believe that she was able to understand. When I said, "Mom," she opened her eyes and looked at me. And this small interaction – this connection between us that I've never experienced before, shook me.

During those seven weeks, I shed many tears, as I ruminated

about the could-have-beens and should-have-beens. I knew that she was approaching the end of her life, unable to speak, cognitively impaired, and unable to give me the closure that I had sought from her my entire life.

Instead, I was left with our last conversation, two weeks prior to my cousin's phone call. Like every other conversation, this one was combative. These were my last words: "I'm so tired of this, mom. Call me back when you don't want to argue with me." Then I hung up the phone. I often wonder how this conversation might have ended, if I had known that this would be our final conversation – the last time I would hear her voice. I will never know.

After a seven-week, bravely-fought battle to survive, my mother died early Friday morning, on September 26th, 1997. I still remember the phone call at 3:30 am. Stella called me, sobbing, "Mom just died." Within the momentary gap of silence following her words, there was a heaviness that seem to engulf the both of us. Even though we knew this was coming, there was still a sense of disbelief. Then she said, "I'll call you later so we can talk about making the arrangements."

I hung up the phone, took a deep breath, and, through a sudden burst of tears, I said to my husband Kenny: "My... mother... just... died." Although I heard myself saying these words, amid the dead silence of the early morning hours, I still couldn't process them yet.

As if a dam had suddenly broken, my tears turned into sobs, and a lifetime of memories forced their way into my thoughts. I felt sad – angry – guilty. I felt cheated out of the closure that I had always fantasized about. I never thought about how I would feel on the day that she died. As illogical as this sounds, I'd always envisioned my mother as being immortal.

Our shared lifetime battles had become such an integral part of my identity. And now, poof — she was gone. I felt as if a part of me – a huge part of me – had also died along with her. I was shocked to find I didn't know how I would be able to live without this piece of myself. Who was I, now that she was gone? It took quite a while before I was able to re-define myself, and identify myself apart from my relationship with my mother and her opinions of me.

Some people say that they experience closure when a contentious, disappointing relationship has ended due to death. Unfortunately, this didn't happen for me. My mom's death didn't extinguish any of the unresolved feelings and the the pain that were such integral parts of our relationship, and my identity. Although death ended our physical relationship, it didn't end the feelings and memories attached to it.

More importantly, it didn't erase the devastating words that I was about to face in the form of her *last will and testament*. These were words written in stone. Words that would stay with me forever.

Chapter 5
Written in Stone

NOT LONG AFTER MY MOTHER'S BURIAL, issues regarding her *last will & testament* began to surface, and become the focus of attention. Like my adoption, apparently everybody in the family, including my sister, knew exactly what was in this will. That is – everyone except me.

Since my Aunt Teri knew I was going to be upset when I learned the details, she gave me a head's up, but she also prefaced this information by saying that my mother intended to amend her will, but never got around to doing so. I will always appreciate and be grateful for the loving support from my aunt.

While my aunt was trying to comfort me, my sister took the opposite approach. She refused to give me a copy of the will, and ignored all of my phone calls. As a result, I was forced to hire an attorney, and pay nearly $1,000, to get a copy from her.

What did I find within that was so shocking and upsetting? These explosive words, which will never be erased from my mind: *"To my daughter, Nella Coiro, I bequeath the sum of one dollar."*

Do I really believe that my mother intended to amend her will? I desperately want to, but I just can't. It doesn't make sense. Each time I revisit this, and I've done so multiple times over the last two decades, I still come to the same upsetting conclusion.

My mother was retired, and had a lot of free time. Every week, she found the time to have her hair done, to go shopping, to go to doctor appointments, and to visit my sister.

At least once, she managed to carve out the time needed to

travel from her house, to the town where my sister lived, and where the attorney was located – a distance of 24 miles. Then, my mother had the time to sit down, and explain to the attorney exactly what she wanted in her will.

People make time for things that they feel are important. Although it's still so painful to accept, this is why I believe she had no intention of amending her will. She had four years – 1,460 *days*, and yet, never found the time to do so.

It has been nearly 25 years since my mother's passing, and my disinheritance still upsets me. Time has not eased the pain. Although I threw away my copy of her will, those words are tattooed in my mind, because they reflect her final wishes, and, with them, her sentiments toward me. My mother was a lot of things, but *stupid* wasn't one of them. She knew exactly what she was doing, and the future repercussions of her actions.

During the four years between the writing of her will, and her death, although we had our periodic quibbles, we were getting along much better, which makes her decision to cut me out of her will even more baffling. Then again, if I think about her vindictive nature, I really shouldn't be so surprised. She lived by these words: "Don't get mad. Get even." Did I think I should've been exempt because I was her daughter? But, then again, I was adopted. I wonder if that made a difference to her.

It's interesting that her will was written the same year I discovered that I was adopted. Although we struggled, I truly believed we got past this. I forgave her. More importantly, during those four years, we talked on the phone, we visited one another, we spent holidays together, and I had absolutely no clue – no indication that this was going to happen.

I often wonder how she was able to look into my eyes, and pretend that nothing was wrong, knowing what she wrote in her will, and knowing the pain this would cause; although, I guess, a sadist could easily do this. Even if she disinherited me impulsively, in a moment of anger, she still had four years — 1,460 days, to change her mind. She didn't. This decision was intentional, and written in stone.

To be clear, I wasn't interested in getting my mother's money or material items. There was nothing of monetary value she had that I couldn't buy for myself. It was never about what she bequeathed. Rather, it was about her sentiments – the anger and the hate – the venom that these 12 words expressed. It felt like my mother sent me the most heinous message possible from the afterlife.

Sometimes I ask myself, *Did she ever love me?*, especially since I had so much evidence to the contrary. Since she physically assaulted me more than once, and relentlessly verbally abused me, I'm convinced that she never cared about me. She never loved me, and she certainly didn't like me. I believe that she was sorry that she adopted me, and she just tolerated me, because she was stuck with me.

My mother wanted me to be an enabler, like Stella. Even when she criticized me, she wanted compliance and agreement, often saying, "Ain't I right?" I just couldn't placate my mother, at my own expense. However, I felt that I was respectful, even in my disagreement. But my definition of *respectful* differed from my mother's. In her mind, if you didn't agree with her 100%, then you were being disrespectful.

I am not sure if my mother had the capacity to love anyone. But what about hate? It's one thing to be apathetic, but it's another thing to hate someone. Did she really hate me that much? All of her actions indicated that the answer was an emphatic "Yes!"

However, for a brash woman, it's interesting that she took a cowardly and sneaky approach regarding this issue. I would have had more respect for her if she told me that she was disinheriting me, and explained the reasons why. A simple explanation like this would have sufficed: "I'm not leaving you anything, because we never got along, and your sister did a lot for me." Although I would have felt hurt, I would have understood.

However, my mother was toxic and vindictive. This type of approach would have been inconceivable to her. She was incapable of approaching this in a healthy way. She wanted me to be shocked and hurt, after she died. She accomplished this, but did she really win? She wasn't here to see the outcome.

I still remember the day I received a letter from her attorney. At the time, I was on crutches, because I had fractured my foot. The doorbell rang, and the postal worker had a certified letter that needed my signature. I signed it, and hobbled inside to open it.

I tore open the envelope to find a crisp, brand-new one dollar bill, and a letter from her attorney saying that this was my inheritance. My whole body began to tremble, I felt nauseated, and suddenly my head began to pound. Even though I knew this was going to happen, it still shook me.

There was something about the physical dollar bill that really upset me, because it felt like such a personal assault. The symbolism was so foul. My total worth to my mother was one hundred cents, and not a penny more. There's nothing that you can buy for a dollar anymore – not even a cup of coffee or a candy bar. And that was my worth to her. *Nothing.*

I can imagine my mother sitting in her attorney's office, telling him to put this information in her will. I wonder if she gave him an explanation as to why she was doing this. If so, this explanation wasn't written in the will.

Knowing my sister's greedy personality, I believe that she was an instigator who influenced my mother's decision to disinherit me. I can envision her sitting right next to my mother, offering her moral support and encouragement. My loss would ultimately become her gain.

Regardless of my sister's influence and scheming, the blame – the responsibility for putting these words in the will falls solely upon my mother. No one forced her to make this decision.

To this day, I wonder if my mother had any idea how deeply these words would hurt me. Did she realize that this pain would haunt me for the rest of my life? And, if so, was that her intention? I can only speculate, but I believe so.

It's weird how some traumatic memories transcend time. The pain and the energy of these recollections have floated through the years, maintaining the same intensity now that they had decades ago. Perhaps it's my fault, and I'm still giving them the power to upset me. If so, I don't know what I can tell my wounded heart, that will allow it to heal and move beyond this trauma.

As I write this chapter, I can still feel my heart pounding, and my eyes tearing up. I don't think the pain of this experience will ever go away. If time really does heal all wounds, this must be the exception. There are some situations in life that we never get over, we just simply carry on in spite of them, as best as possible. This is one of those circumstances.

Over the last few decades, I've thought about our relationship, and wondered why she wasn't able to muster up even the smallest amount of warmth and support toward me. Did she lack the capacity to do so? Was it something about me, personally? Was it because I wasn't her biological daughter?

Although I knew that my mom was combative with nearly

everyone around her, especially if they disagreed with her, her mistreatment of me still felt personal. It always felt like she wanted to have a relationship with me, even though she didn't like anything about me. I just couldn't understand this.

And then, her words in her Will, written in stone with indelible ink, shouted at me, a re-affirmation that she didn't just dislike me, she hated me. There are no words that can erase this fact, or soothe this pain.

Chapter 6
In Pitch-Black Darkness

THE AFTERMATH OF LEARNING about my mother's sentiments in her will was devastating. I felt lost, and immersed in a deep realm of blinding darkness. I felt as if I was trapped in a pitch-black room without any doors or exits. During this time, it was nearly impossible to function. It took a great deal of energy to do my routine, day-to-day activities, including simple tasks like taking a shower, eating, and concentrating.

While my sister changed her phone number, and abruptly ended all contact with me, my Aunt Teri and my cousin Joanna were supportive, and tried to comfort me. Although I greatly appreciated this, there was nothing that could soothe or heal this gaping wound.

In *The Divine Comedy*, as Dante approaches the gates of Hell (L'inferno), he reads an inscription that warns him about what Hell is going to be like. After my mother's death, followed by the disinheritance, I found myself identifying with each of these adjectives he used:

"Through me, you enter the city of woe.
Through me, you enter eternal grief.
Through me, you enter among the lost.
Abandon any hope, all you who enter."

I felt all of the above: anguish, with no end in sight – I felt lost – I felt hopeless. I was grieving so many losses, and shedding endless tears. I was deeply immersed in Hell. I didn't think that I would ever exit from this chilling darkness, or feel the warm comfort of sunlight ever again.

I couldn't focus on anything, except for the fact that my mother hated me. *She really freakin' hated me.* I knew we had our differences. But this? There was simply no way that I could spin this to make it sound any better than the harsh reality. It was so icy cold. I could feel the hate coming from beyond the grave.

To further exacerbate the situation, my sister continued to pour gasoline on the fire that my mother had created. She went to my mother's condo, removed all of her personal effects, kept most of them, and sold whatever she didn't want. She didn't offer one thing to me. Besides this, she ignored all of my phone calls, and eventually changed her phone number. I was shocked that I was disinherited, but equally shocked by my sister's cold and heartless actions.

Amid this hopeless darkness, many thoughts crossed my mind. I wondered what my father would've thought if he were alive. I believe that he would have considered her actions appalling. He had his issues, but he wasn't hateful or vindictive.

As I reflected upon her final hateful act towards me, I relived the assaults she inflicted upon me over the years:

- The black eye and swollen lip she gave me when I was in kindergarten.
- The bar of soap she shoved into my mouth when I was about eight, because I uttered a profanity.
- The knife she held to my throat a few weeks before I got married, threatening to kill me because I disagreed with her.
- The rage she had toward *me* when I discovered that I was adopted, as though *she* was the offended party.
- And the constant ongoing bullying, criticizing, and verbal abuse.

And yet, I've never been able to permanently walk away from this relationship. Why? Because she was my mother, and despite all of the abuse, and all of the ongoing conflicts, a part of me still loved her. There really isn't any other explanation.

Chapter 7
Kindergarten

M Y EARLIEST MEMORY DATES BACK to when I was five years old, and I was going to kindergarten. I was being taken somewhere outside of my house, and outside of my comfort zone, and I was unhappy and afraid. The elementary school, PS32, was a block away, within walking distance. This school housed grades kindergarten to eighth grade.

From my young, five-year-old perspective, I was being brought to a big, scary building, and left there with people I didn't know. I was terrified of being abandoned. In fact, I've had abandonment issues my entire life.

It was the 1960's, and words like *separation anxiety* didn't exist yet. However, I was given a couple of identifying labels: *withdrawn* and *painfully shy*. I didn't really understand what these descriptors meant, but I knew they weren't good, and they seemed to indicate that there was something wrong with me.

On the first day of school, my mother held my hand, and as we walked up the street, I could see the school from a distance – a huge, ominous red-brick building. Minutes after entering the building, a middle-aged woman with short, gray hair, met us at the foot of a stairway. I remember the staircase, enclosed by what looked like a silver cage, which extended upward from the banister toward the ceiling.

The air was filled with the faint, waxy aroma of Crayola crayons. This was comforting and familiar, because I associated crayons with fun. At the same time, it was quiet, absent of any muffled sounds of other children, and this frightened me. I thought, *if this is a school, where are the other kids?* Added to this, when my mother and the teacher spoke to one another, their voices seem to loudly reverberate throughout the hallway, and bounce off the walls. This frightened me as well.

As my mother let go of my hand, and told me to go with the teacher, who I saw as a scary stranger, I began to sob. I tightly clung to my mother's leg, emphatically shaking my head, "no." She continued to push me, saying, "It's okay, Nell. You can go with this nice lady and play with the other kids." But I was strong-willed, even at that age, and I was too afraid to do as she asked.

Despite my mother's prompts to go with the teacher, I couldn't stop crying, so we went home. As soon as we were out of the building, my mother yanked my hand, and sighed. She said, "God damn it! Why are you so difficult? I just don't understand you." Her anger just increased my fear.

We repeated this same scenario for a couple of days, as my mother's exasperation and anger increased. Finally, at the suggestion of the teacher, my mother enlisted my maternal grandfather to take me to school. I liked my grandfather, I wasn't afraid of him, and apparently I didn't have the same attachment toward him, because I didn't burst into tears when he accompanied me. This time, I quietly went with the teacher.

Maybe I didn't associate him with abuse, or the fear of being abandoned. I can only speculate that, from an early age, I had contradictory feelings toward my mother. I was terrified of her, and a part of that terror was the fear of being abandoned by her. I wouldn't be surprised if this fear developed because sometimes she threatened to leave me somewhere, if I didn't comply with her demands.

Eventually, I began to enjoy kindergarten. I remember

snippets of fragmented memories: coloring books, crayons, and finger painting projects. Over time, my fears subsided, and I became more comfortable being around other children.

At the end of the year, it was customary to take an individual photograph of each student, as well as a group photo. In this picture, I'm wearing a pink dress, my right eye is bruised and my lip is swollen. I still have this photograph, and every time I look at it, I feel sad for that helpless little girl.

What happened? According to my mother's explanation, she was trying to curl my hair, and I hid under the kitchen table. During the ensuing commotion, I injured myself, as I tried to get away from her. She said that eventually I conceded, and I let her curl my hair.

Vaguely, I remember a kerfuffle, where she dragged me from underneath the table. I don't remember what happened next. However, knowing her temper, and the fact that she struck me at other times, I find it hard to believe that these injuries were incurred because I banged my face and lip against the table leg. Rather, in my photo, it looks as if I was punched by a closed fist.

Since teachers are now mandated reporters, if this happened today, Child Protective Services would have been notified. However, CPS didn't exist back then. Still, I wonder what the teacher thought when she saw the bruises, and if she really believed my mother's explanation.

I also wonder how my five-year-old mind connected and processed these two events; First, the initial fear of going to kindergarten, which I perceived as a frightening place; second, the fact that my mother beat me before I had a photograph taken at the end of the school year. I was afraid to go to kindergarten in the beginning, and then eventually I felt safe and comfortable, and I enjoyed being there. And then, at the end of this experience,

I must have associated being unexpectedly assaulted with the kindergarten experience.

It's not surprising that these early feelings were a thread that followed me throughout my life. I had ongoing, conflicting feelings toward my mother. My abandonment issues never subsided, or even lessened. To this day, I still have ongoing nightmares with the abandonment theme. I grew used to the fear of losing anyone who was important to me. I also became guarded and learned to take a defensive position, because my mother instilled in me the fear of unexpected physical violence.

Chapter 8
Little Italy

I GREW UP IN THE BELMONT AVENUE-187th Street section of the Bronx, in NY. The area was dubbed the Little Italy of the Bronx, because most of the residents were either Italian immigrants, or of Italian-American descent.

The neighborhood gained some notoriety because it was the home of the musical group, Dion and the Belmonts, as well as actors Joe Pesci and Chazz Palminteri. In fact, the movie, *A Bronx Tale*, written by Chazz Palminteri, was based upon his childhood in the neighborhood. In addition, some scenes from the *The Godfather* movie were filmed on Arthur Avenue, in Mario's Restaurant.

Even today, Arthur Avenue is well known for its Italian markets, bakeries, pastry shops, delicatessens, fish markets, cafes, novelty shops, and authentic Italian restaurants. People still travel from other neighborhoods, and out-of-state, to shop and eat there.

Other popular attractions include two annual Italian festivals, called *feasts*. When I was growing up, they were hosted by Our Lady of Mount Carmel Church. A feast is like a huge block party, that extends about eight blocks.

Back when I was a child, the feasts had carnival games, live musical entertainment, rides, and delicious Italian foods like sausage and peppers, pizza, calzones, zeppoli, and Italian ices. The coffee shops lining the streets would serve espressos and frothy cappuccinos, made from freshly ground coffee beans. The large, life-sized statue of the Blessed Mother was paraded throughout the feast, and parishioners would pin money onto the statue, which was later donated to the church.

In the 1960's, some of the terminology we used to describe our world, also differed from today. We didn't use the word *community*. We referred to the area in which we lived as *the neighborhood*. We didn't say the word *street* when referencing where we lived. *Streets* were called *blocks*.

We also said, *"Up the block"* or *"Down the block."* This had nothing to do with north and south, however. *Down the block* always meant we were walking from our street, toward 187th Street, which was where all the stores were located. (I know how confusing and logical this sounds, but it made perfect sense to us.) If we walked *up the block*, there were two candy stores on either end of our street – Moe's and Kitty's. To clarify, a candy store in those days was actually a luncheonette.

Luncheonettes sold sandwiches, hotdogs, burgers, and beverages like fountain sodas, soft drinks, tea, and coffee. They were also known for making egg-creams, which were cold drinks with milk, chocolate syrup and seltzer. Egg-creams are tasty, and are still popular. (Although they're called egg-creams, they don't contain eggs or cream.)

These stores also sold candies like Bazooka bubble gum, jaw-breakers, licorice, Mary Janes, chocolate cigarettes, candy dots attached to paper, Turkish taffy, and Hershey chocolate kisses. There was also ice cream, stick pretzels, and huge wooden barrels with large, mouth-watering pickles. Sadly, luncheonettes are much rarer these days. They've mostly been replaced by diners and fast food chains.

There were also a few pizzerias in our neighborhood. On 187th St., there was Half Moon Pizzeria, which had the best pizza in the area, with crispy crust, and a flavorful homemade sauce. During the feasts, Half Moon had an outdoor stand, where pizza was served from a large tin warmer. There was also another noteworthy pizzeria on Arthur Avenue, called Catania's. Their slices were oblong, and had a unique taste, because they were made with a different type of pizza dough.

Throughout the neighborhood, there were several Italian cafes that sold espresso, cappuccino, and Italian pastries. Some of the cafes housed a jukebox, a pool table, or a TV, so the customers could watch soccer games and other sports. Most of these shops were frequented by men, and often, this was where the mobsters hung out. Some cafes were also known for *taking numbers* – placing illegal bets with bookies, from which the mafia took a percentage.

Our street had one and two-family houses, and several large buildings. I lived in a pale green, aluminum-sided, two-family house, with a small front yard, enclosed by hedges, a front porch, and a big backyard with a large patio, and a fig tree. My father loved that fig tree! Every day, he would water the fig tree, and pick ripe figs, which were sweet and delicious. In the winter, he'd cover the tree with a dark green tarp. Other than that, my parents didn't go into the backyard to sit or entertain, but my sister and I would go there to play.

When my parents weren't in the basement, during the summer evenings, they would sit on the green and white metal recliner on the front porch, so they could "see what's going on in the neighborhood," and chat with the neighbors next-door, who were also sitting on their front porch.

Most of my mother's family lived across the street, in a red-brick, two-family house, with a basement apartment. This included my grandfather, my Aunt Teri, my Uncle Mike, my Aunt Rita (who was a widow), and my four cousins: Sal, Joanna, Phil, and Theresa. We spent all of holidays with my mother's family, and my paternal grandparents.

My mother's brother, Sal, who was a draftsman, lived in his own home, with his wife Dorothy, a stay-at-home mom, and my three cousins, twins Maria and Angela, and their younger sister, Monique. Since they didn't live on our street, we saw them less often. My paternal grandparents lived in a building about four blocks away.

Other than family, my parents socialized with siblings Johnny and Carmina, who were both single, and lived next-door with their parents, Nikki and Louie. Johnny was in his 40's, had salt and pepper hair, wore a pinky ring, and was nicknamed *Crazy Johnny*. I'm not sure exactly why he had this nickname. Johnny was constantlsy pestering my parents to cosign his loans, though they always declined, and warned us that we should never co-sign loans. When he wasn't scheming, he was working on his car.

Carmina was an attractive woman in her mid-30's, with short, reddish-brown hair, and a pleasant personality. Her job involved interacting with out-of-state salesmen, and she dated some of them, uncaring of the fact that they were married. Often, she invited some of them to her house for dinner, and sometimes she introduced them to my parents.

She often spent time at our house, especially on Saturdays, when she and my mother had their hair done. Sometimes she helped my mother with housework. Other times, she flirted with my father, and he reciprocated, while my mother ignored their exchanges. The conversations were pretty risqué for the 1960's, full of sexual innuendo that was impossible to excuse as innocent.

Carl was the hairdresser in the neighborhood, and he made house calls. Every Saturday, Carl would come to our house to perform his work. My mother seemed to be the happiest when she was having her hair done. This was the highlight of her week, and she never canceled her appointment.

Carl was a charming, tall man in his 30s, and he wore eyeglasses. Carl had some sort of medical condition which rendered him bald, so he wore a light brown wig that looked fake. I think it helped him to feel more comfortable with himself.

Everyone seemed to know that Carl was gay. Sadly, he lived during a time when gay people were in danger, and afraid to come out. Like other gay men in the 1960s, Carl married a woman and had children, to protect his secret. He often spoke about how his wife didn't trust him, and that sometimes she would check on his whereabouts.

While my mother and Carmina were having their hair done, my parents would play, and laugh at Pat Cooper albums. Most Italians loved Pat Cooper, a popular comedian at the time, who talked about life as an Italian-American. The hairdressing ritual was one of the only times when I saw my mother crack a smile. My parents refrained from arguing, when Carl was doing my mother's hair, or when Carmina or Johnny were visiting.

It's interesting that I never heard my parents mock or speak badly about Carl, especially during such a homophobic era. To them, he was simply a talented hair stylist, and a charming guy of Italian-American descent, who also enjoyed Pat Cooper.

Chapter 9
The Family

*L*IKE MOST PEOPLE, my parents were complicated, and composed of many layers. I believe they both had unresolved childhood issues which contributed to who they became as adults. Their troubled relationship with one another also changed them, and gradually morphed into how they conducted themselves as parents.

My mother, who everyone referred to as Vinni (even though her first name was Maria), was about 5'2", and an attractive woman, with blonde hair, blue eyes, and a light complexion. She resembled her own mother quite a bit. She was first generation American, born of Italian immigrants, and bilingual. Since it was unusual to see Italians with blue eyes and blonde hair, people often thought that she was Irish or German.

She struggled with her weight her entire life, and she was always on some sort of a diet, most frequently Weight Watchers, and periodically, she took diet pills. Although, or perhaps, since she was obese, she was extremely preoccupied with her appearance. She would never consider leaving the house without wearing make-up and jewelry, and she often criticized me because I didn't share this obsession. "Nell, fix yourself up," she would say. "At least put on some makeup before you go out."

She was also fanatical about wearing clean underwear, which I thought was a bit weird. She would say, "You must always remember to change your underwear every day. What would happen if you were sick or unconscious, and an ambulance had to take you to the hospital? Wouldn't you be embarrassed if you weren't wearing clean underwear?" The ambulance she often talked about never came.

My maternal grandfather worked in construction as a brick-layer, and my grandmother was a homemaker. I remember my grandfather as tall, with thinning gray hair. He had a *toothbrush mustache* similar to those sported by Oliver Hardy and Charlie Chaplin, and he smoked little thin, brown cigars nicknamed "skinny stinkers." He was a man of few words, who was witty at times, and made his own wine. He was also proud of the fact that, at 84 years old, he still had all of his original teeth, often smiling, and pointing at them, to give everyone a look.

My grandfather was also a generous man. Every year, to cele-brate his birthday, he gave one dollar to each of his nine grand-children. Today, this would be equivalent to about ten dollars each. We would line up according to our age, and my sister, who was the youngest grandchild, was at the front of the line.

I never met my maternal grandmother, who died before I was born. In photos, she appeared to be an attractive woman. Sadly, she was ill most of her life, hospitalized frequently, and then cared for by my aunts. She suffered from severe hyperten-sion, and, unfortunately, she lived during a time before blood pressure medications existed. I've heard stories of leeches being put on her to lower her blood pressure.

My grandmother died when she was 47 years old, and my grandfather, who was 57, never remarried. From what I was told, she was a warm and kind woman. She also loved nurses, because she was grateful for the loving care that they gave her when she was hospitalized. Therefore, she and my grandfather saved what little money they had, so that they could send their eldest daughter, my Aunt Rita, to nursing school.

My mother was 24 years old when her mother died, and I

know she never recovered from the premature death of her mother, because she often spoke about how much she missed her. Although my mother rarely showed her emotions, often she shed tears when she spoke about her mother, who she called "mama." There was a popular song by Connie Francis, called *Mama*, and my mother would cry whenever she heard it, and sometimes she would sing along, because she said that it reminded her of her own mother.

Out of curiosity, I googled the translated lyrics of this song, and a few lyrics struck me: "Safe in the glow of your love, sent from the heavens above. Nothing can ever replace the warmth of your tender embrace."

I have this question: *If* indeed my grandmother was like the woman in the song, a tender, loving mother, then what happened to my mother? How does a woman who was *mothered* by such a kind-hearted person, become the frightening, abusive woman I remember as my mother? How did my mother become a cold-hearted person who never expressed affection, never hugged her own children, and never said the words, "I love you?" The contrast is staggering.

I don't know a great deal about my grandfather's personality when he was young. From what I could gather, he was strict, short-tempered, and somewhat stubborn. Perhaps my mother inherited some of his characteristics.

Aside from the shocking contrast between my mother and my grandmother, since my mother also had hypertension, she was always afraid that she would die at the same age as my grandmother, and often spoke about this fear. She stopped verbalizing this fear when she lived beyond 47 years old.

My father was also bi-lingual, and the son of Italian immigrants. He was thin, about 5'9"in height, he had curly black hair, a dark complexion, and a great personality. Since he wasn't a very attractive man, I often wondered why my mother married him, when she was so obsessed with physical appearance. When she met him, he was missing most of his teeth, because his parents never brought him to a dentist when he was a child. How sad is that?

After they were married, he finally went to a dentist, had his remaining decayed teeth removed, and he got full dentures. But he also had other medical issues. For example, he had nose surgery because he had a deviated septum, and he had several ongoing surgeries for bleeding ulcers.

Since my father was Sicilian, and he had an extremely dark complexion, he was often mistaken for a man of African, or of Latin-American descent. At times, some of the racist Italians in the neighborhood who didn't know him, assumed that he was a Black man, and they thought they had the right to walk by our house, and call him a *moulinyan*. This word is considered a racial slur, equivalent to the N-word.

Typical comments were, "Hey, moulinyan, get out of the neighborhood. We don't want you here." Or, "Go live with your own kind." Other people thought he was Latino, and would say, "Go back to Puerto Rico." Sometimes he ignored these comments, and other times he would get angry, and respond, "First of all, I'm Italian. Second, even if I was Puerto Rican or Colored, what makes you think you have the right to say that to me? Vaffanculo!" (Translation: Go fuck yourself!)

He was always upset by these hateful comments, and often told my sister and I that we should never judge people by their skin color, or speak to anyone in this cruel way. For all his faults, and he had a few, he wasn't a racist, and I never heard him make racist comments. This is probably because he experienced racism firsthand.

Being mistreated and bullied wasn't new to my father. He had a terribly abusive childhood. When he was eleven years old, he was forced to assume the role of the breadwinner to support his family, because his father wasn't in love with the idea of working for a living. His father would get into fistfights with co-workers and bosses, and he couldn't keep a job for long. He was simply lazy. However, he was also a charming man, and he loved to socialize, as long as it didn't involve doing any actual work.

And yet, this same man who brutalized my father, was a fairly decent grandfather. I remember him as a kind man, who was nearly six-feet tall, with gray balding hair, and he wore eyeglasses. I enjoyed spending time with him, and we shared a love of animals. He took me to the Bronx Zoo a few times, and talked to me about the animals there. I wonder what happened to made him transition from an abusive father to a kind grandfather.

In contrast, my paternal grandmother, who had gray hair, worn as a bun, was an impatient, irritable woman, who didn't like kids, and lacked warmth. My sister and I dreaded going to her house. She would point at my sister and I, and say, in her strong Italian accent: "shut uppa you mouth," "seeta down," "no talka too much," or "play weeta you toyza." In other words, she wanted us to be invisible, and refrain from annoying her in any way.

As mentioned, when my father was a child, he was severely abused by both of his parents. There were times when they locked him in a closet for days, beat him, and refused to feed him. He didn't receive even an iota of warmth, affection, or love from them. Rather, they looked upon him as a burden, and they felt that he existed solely to serve them. In many ways, they didn't see him as a human being with feelings. It's sad that he chose to marry a woman who was also abusive toward him, and treated him similarly to how he was treated by his parents.

Despite my father's abusive childhood, he never expressed resentment or negative feelings toward his parents. Still, I imagine he must have had some feelings about this. I believe that he repressed all of his anger, hurt, and disappointment, which resulted in stress-related illnesses like stomach ulcers, as well as toxic behavior.

During his childhood, he discovered that the woman he thought was his biological mother, was actually his common-law stepmother. He learned this from neighbors who knew my grandfather when he lived in Ohio. Yet, he never told his parents that he discovered this information.

Apparently, my grandfather abandoned his wife and his other children, and, without his wife's consent, he took my father, who was his eldest son. He relocated, and, at some point, he met the woman I knew as my grandmother, who grew up in an orphanage, and never knew her parents or her family. If my father didn't learn this information, he would have continued to believe that his step-mother was his biological mother.

On my grandfather's deathbed, he legally married my grandmother. After his death, she moved into our house. She was disruptive and intrusive. At night, she would walk into my parent's bedroom without knocking, and insist upon giving her son a massage, and wanted him to reciprocate. Several times, my parents asked her not to go into their bedroom, but she continued to do so. Eventually, to stop this, my parents put a huge, deadbolt lock on their bedroom door.

My grandmother also wanted my father to bathe her, as he apparently did when he lived with his parents, before he was married. Clearly, they had boundary issues, and an inappropriate and incestuous relationship.

My grandmother's presence increased the tension in an already turbulent atmosphere, and the arguments between my parents increased. My mother would argue, "Your mother shouldn't be coming into our bedroom and trying to massage you, or asking you to bathe her. That's sick."

My mother wanted my father to put his mother in a nursing home, but he protested, "That's terrible. You just don't do that to your mother." My father was usually passive, but he adamantly refused to comply regarding this issue.

My grandmother lived with us for a few years, until she passed away. Her belongings included statues of the Blessed Mother and Jesus, a pair of rosary beads, and some photos. Among her possessions, my father found a photo that he never knew existed. It was a photograph of his biological mother, and his other siblings. He was stunned and saddened to see that he looked exactly like his birth mom, and he spent his entire adult life wondering about the whereabouts of his birth mother, and his other siblings.

My father wore many hats. Outwardly, he was the guy who went out of his way to help others, and he was particularly talented at both home and auto repairs. *Need a favor, or need something fixed? Call Jimmy.* He had an amicable, warm personality, a good sense of humor, and presented himself as a happy, carefree, family man. He desperately wanted to be liked by everyone.

However, my father had darker side. He was a troubled, unhappy man, often depressed, and he lived with pent-up feelings of anger, frustration, and low self-esteem. He lived a mundane life, where he worked 50 to 60 hours a week, then came home and watched television. He was a member of a weekly bowling league, where he won many trophies, and he also liked to play pool, and read books.

He was also envious, and he often vocalized his jealousy concerning family members, especially my Uncle Mike. I heard him say, "I walked in the house, and Mike didn't even look up to say hello. He was eating his steak like a dog chewing on a bone." Sometimes, referring to my aunt and uncle, he would say: "Look at them. They have all the luck. Why can't we catch a break?"

In different ways, both of my parents had stressful childhoods. My mother grew up with the stress of living with a strict, unyielding father, and caring for her seriously ill mother, who died prematurely. Since she and her sisters took care their mother, they were unable to experience stress-free childhoods. My mother was also jealous of the fact that her sister Rita was chosen over her to go to nursing school. Aside from missing her, I don't know any personal details regarding my mother's relationship with her mother.

Since my father's childhood was severely toxic because of the verbal, physical and sexual abuse that he suffered, he was left with some severe psychological issues. I often wonder if my mother had any idea what she was signing up for. At the same time, I wonder if he knew beforehand that my mother had a domineering, abusive personality.

When two people with unresolved childhood issues get married and have a family, their issues are going to affect their children. This is known as *generational trauma*, and it's exactly what happened. In that era, shameful issues were denied and never spoken about. It was unthinkable to criticize parents. Besides this, most Italians didn't go to therapists.

"Only crazy people go to psychiatrists." This was my mother's belief. She wasn't alone. In the 1960's, many people of Italian-American heritage frowned upon the idea of seeing a psychiatrist. If you had a serious problem, you would talk to the local priest.

They believed that only those with serious psychiatric issues, *crazy people*, would see a psychiatrist or a psychologist. My mother took it one step further. Aside from believing that only *crazy* people went to psychiatrists, she also thought that the psychiatrists themselves were a little bit crazy, rationalizing, "They have to be crazy. Why else would they want to deal with crazy people?" This made perfect sense to her, and my father shared her sentiments.

A part of the rigid Italian taboo was that you should never tell strangers any family business. Anything that happens within the family must be kept within the family. There are no exceptions. My mother would often repeat, "Don't ever tell strangers what happens in our family. That's our personal business." This was the number one rule in our house.

Although there was a lot of craziness happening in my family, my parents never saw themselves as crazy. But they were often the first to diagnose the mental health and moral character of everyone around them.

Speaking to my father, out of nowhere, my mother made this observation about our next door neighbor: "Jimmy, don't you think Johnny's a little mental?" (She used the word *mental* to denote mental illness.)

My father agreed: "*E'pazzo*. He's mental like his father. Probably can't help it. Poor guy. But his sister... *una puttana*. What a slut... Shameful... Her father is so strict. It's OK his daughter goes out with married men?"

My mother weighed in, "Maybe he doesn't understand she's probably sleeping with them."

My father continued his observations, "Could he be that stupid?"

"Probably," My mother laughed.

Somehow, they never thought there was a possibility that they might be *mental* – maybe even more than *Crazy Johnny*. On the contrary, they saw themselves as normal, or, as my mother put it, "well-adjusted." And yet, they both had serious mental health and substance abuse issues, especially mood disorders.

My mother was often depressed. She would explain this by saying, "I don't feel good." Maybe she didn't feel well, but she never would have identified what she was feeling as depression, because, in doing so, she would have to see *herself* as *mental*. In her eyes, only crazy people got depressed.

Depressed or not, she was always anxious and irritable, and it was always someone else's fault. "Stop aggravating me," was her usual request, even when no one was actually aggravating her.

I know, without a doubt, that my father suffered from depression, and he might have been bipolar. When he was depressed, he was quiet, he avoided interacting with the rest of the family, and he was easily brought to tears. My father cried often, and whenever he did, it upset me a great deal.

When his mood shifted, he displayed different types of manic behavior, which included a serious issue with gambling and, according to my mother, hyper-sexuality. After his death, my mother revealed that my father was constantly interested in sex, and she felt guilty because often she "refused him." My father had a lot of issues concerning his sexuality, and he transitioned from being a victim of incest, to being a perpetrator of incest.

My father also had drinking issues. He drank beer – a lot of beer, possibly to self-medicate. I'm guessing that he was desperately trying to escape his emotional pain, his predatory behavior, and the cesspool of negativity that he created and swam in. He was a closet drinker, and never drank in front of extended family members.

There were times when he drank so much that he lost consciousness, and fell off his chair. My mother justified this by saying that he didn't pass out because of his excessive drinking. Rather, that my father worked hard, and he was simply tired, and fell asleep.

My mother never drank alcohol, but she developed a strong love affair with Valium. In the 1960's, Valium was a newly FDA-approved benzodiazepine which became popular among women. Doctors were writing prescriptions faster than the pharmacies could fill them.

The Rolling Stones even wrote a hit song about this tranquilizer, called *Mother's Little Helper*, somewhat tongue in cheek, yet asserting: Women, do you need something to calm your nerves? Voila! – there's a little yellow pill that can do just that!

Since my mother told her doctor that she was "very nervous and stressed," he happily gave her a prescription for Valium, and she soon discovered that this medication could quickly *calm her nerves*. Yet, she never referred to her problem as *anxiety*, because again, this would imply that she was *mental*. She also didn't view Valium as an addicting or dangerous drug, because her doctor prescribed it.

In my house, Valium should have been put in the candy dishes, because the pill popping happened at a rapid speed, completely tossing aside the *used as directed* instructions on the prescription bottle. Every time my mother got nervous (which was most of the time), she quickly reached for her coveted bottle of Valium.

Sometimes she would ask my sister for help, "Stella, Mommy doesn't feel good. Get me my pills right away." (Everyone knew that her *pills* were Valium.) Or, she would blame my father, "Damn it to hell, Jimmy. Stop aggravating me. My heart is fluttering. Now I have to take my pill."

Often, tossing her hands in the air, and sighing, she would blame my sister and me: "Goddamnit! See what you kids did? Aggravating me. Now I need to take *my pills*." No matter who was at fault, my mother always found a reason for taking *her pills*.

My aunts and our next-door neighbor, Carmina, also seemed to over-enjoy this *mother's little helper*, and if they ran out of pills, my mother would share some of hers, and vice versa. They all ignored the warning that medication, any medication, should never be shared.

My mother didn't eat a lot of food, but she loved cakes and sweets, which were high in calories, so she had an ongoing weight problem. Periodically, she took diet pills (amphetamines), which were prescribed by her doctor for weight loss. I think that perhaps her abuse of Valium and amphetamines eventually led to her cardiac issues, or what she called a "heart condition."

It's sad that my father found it acceptable to drink excessively, and my mother thought it was okay to ingest Valiums as if they were Junior mints, yet they never would have considered taking antidepressants, which might have helped them with their mood issues, because this was so taboo in their eyes.

In fact, decades later, when my mother's second husband, Joe, was prescribed antidepressants, she adamantly refused to call them what they actually were. Instead she would refer to them as "happy pills," adding that he had "nothing to be depressed about."

Apparently, semantics were always important, including names. What's in a name? That was a loaded question in my family!

My family was talented at complicating the simplest of situations, especially regarding names. There was particular confusion regarding my mother's name and my own. One of my aunts had a nickname that reflected her personality, but not in a good way. There was also melodrama following the aftermath concerning a cousin's name change.

Everyone in my family called my mother by a different name, yet no one called her by her actual first name. My aunts and uncles called her *Vinni*, which was short for Vincenza, her middle name. Some of my cousins called her Aunt May, and others called her Aunt Mary. She answered to all of these names.

My name also has an interesting story. In Italian families, children were named after one of their grandparents, and I was supposedly named after my paternal grandmother, but... not really. Here's why. My grandmother's name was Annalena, but everyone called her Nellie. Somehow they derived my name – Nella – from her nickname – Nellie.

Although, legally my name is *Nella*, my family members still called me *Nellie*. Every time I've asked how my name, Nella, was derived from my grandmother's name, I've never received a clear explanation.

My Aunt Rita had a well-earned nickname – *the little general.* The *little* part of her title referred to her height. She about five feet tall. The *general* part referred to her demeanor, because she was bossy and rude. In some ways, her personality was similar to my mother's, but she more aggressive and confrontational. Yet, their sister, my Aunt Teri, was the complete opposite. She was kind-hearted, and had a warm and loving personality.

Aunt Rita was a registered nurse, and a supervisor. She behaved as if she was smarter than everyone else, and had the right to tell others how they should behave, according to her specifications. I recall quite a few of her berating and offensive remarks toward me over the years, but do not remember ever hearing one kind word from her.

In fact, there was an incident involving my aunt and my husband's parents, which showed how obnoxious she could be. My mother was in the hospital at the time, and my in-laws took public transportation, and traveled quite a distance, just to visit her. As they attempted to enter my mother's room, my aunt blocked their path, and refused to let them in, rudely telling them, "You can't come in. She's sleeping. Come back another day."

My mother-in-law told me that she peaked into the room, and saw that my mother wasn't asleep; she was eating and watching TV. Abruptly, my aunt closed the door in their faces. This behavior was typical of my aunt – rude, condescending, and behaving as her nickname implied – an unapologetic, obnoxious *general*.

There's another name-related story that is somewhat funny, but it also demonstrates my grandfather's immaturity. When she was a teenager, one of my cousins wanted to change her first name, *Fanny*, because she was upset that the other kids were mocking her. Combining her first and last name, the kids would call her "Fanny Ass." My uncle decided to grant her wishes, and she legally changed her name to Angela.

When my grandfather learned that his granddaughter was going to change her name, which was also the name of his deceased wife, he became enraged, and took this as a personal insult. One day, he figured out a way to retaliate.

My grandfather found a beautiful, feral, black cat, and adopted him. However, he didn't do so because he was much of an animal lover, although he did take good care of this animal. Indirectly, he used this cat to make a point, and to upset my Uncle Sal, and his family.

Since my cousin changed her name to *Angela*, my grandfather decided to purposely name this cat *Angelo*, to mock my cousin's name change. Then he made it his business to let everyone in the family know that he named his cat, Angelo, after my cousin. This was during a time when no one used human names to name their animals.

In Italian families, no one disrespected their elders, so my grandfather knew that he could get away with taunting my uncle and my cousin. No one would have dared to call him out on this, confront him, or point out how immature and ridiculous it was.

During family gatherings, he would say Angelo's name over and over again, to taunt my uncle and my teenage cousin. It was rather funny, but I'm sure my uncle and my cousin didn't think so.

I think that my grandfather was deeply hurt, and his immature behavior, and comments, were his way of irritating my uncle and his family. He just couldn't let this go. Instead, in his mind, because he couldn't control the situation, he was retaliating the only way that he knew how.

My uncle ignored his comments, and I'm sure that he instructed his family to do so too. No one was allowed to argue with or disrespect Pop or grandpa. This was the ultimate rule in Italian families. And so, this nonsense was ignored, and my grandfather probably didn't get the satisfaction that he had hoped for.

Chapter 10
Behind the Snapshots

NAPSHOTS CAPTURE A SECOND IN TIME, and a memory of that particular moment. However, how accurate is that memory? What about the surrounding events, and the other moments that occurred before and after the photo was taken? Snapshots rarely capture any possible negativity that might be a part of the event being photographed, because everyone is instructed to smile, regardless of how they might feel.

As I look at old childhood snapshots, I'm struck by the disparity between what the photos imply, and the actual experiences I remember. I appear happy in most of them, yet, when some of these photos were taken, I can still remember the tears concealed behind the smiles. There are many photos where my sister and I are smiling as we opened gifts. This might've been how the day began, but this wasn't how it progressed. The day often ended with arguing between my parents.

The holidays were always stressful, which makes many of the Christmas photographs misleading, because they didn't reflect the entire story. For example, every year my mother would argue with my father, because she wanted him to install outdoor Christmas lights. "Jimmy, everyone else put up their lights up. We can't be the only house that doesn't have Christmas lights," she would say.

"Why? Who cares?" he retorted, flailing his hands.

"It doesn't look good," she responded.

Since my father hated this task, the annual arguing began: "It's so cold outside! Why do I have to waste my time doing this shit every year?"

He would complain, but ultimately, he conceded. Then he'd be irritable the rest of the day. Nonetheless, my mother compelled him to take photos of the outdoor lights. Although there was no *Christmas joy* inside our house, the outside of the house, including the snapshots, gave a different impression.

There's also an interesting story behind a snapshot taken during Christmas, where my mother, me and my husband, and my sister and her husband, were sitting around a table, eating dinner. My stepfather was taking the photo, so he wasn't in the picture. We were all smiling, yet this photo has an underlying story...

My mother never spoke directly to my husband or my sister's husband. Rather, she directed her remarks toward me and my sister, and expected us to repeat her comments to our husbands – even though they were sitting right in front of her!

She might say, "Nell, does Kenny want more salad?," or, to my sister, "Stella, does Robby want more food?" Often, I would laugh and say, "C'mon mom, they're right here. Why don't you just speak to them directly?" Yet, she would ignore my question, and continued to communicate with them in this ridiculous manner.

I believe that she did this because she had an underlying resentment, since our husbands did not refer to her as "mom." Although they were respectful, since they didn't acknowledge her in the fashion she wanted, she chose to avoid direct communication with them. And so, there was much more to this snapshot than five people sitting around a table, happily eating dinner. Everything happening beneath the photo was hidden.

The most appalling snapshot was my kindergarten photo, where I'm pictured with a black eye and a swollen lip. Clearly, someone beat me and bruised my face. Yet, this tragedy wasn't acknowledged by anyone, and the photo was taken as if nothing had happened. As I look at the photo of this bruised little girl, who is trying so hard to smile, I can see the sadness in her eyes. I wonder what she was thinking.

Although this kindergarten photo isn't as subtle as the others, there is still so much of the story that this simple snapshot isn't telling. Nonetheless, most of my childhood and other family photos also had an underlying story that dwelled behind the snapshots.

Chapter 11
Old Photographs

⟨⟡⟩

THEY SAY YOU CAN TELL A LOT about a person by looking at their photographs. Sometimes those photos, pieced together, tell a visual biography, or a memoir. Often, a single photo can reveal more about a person, than pages of text. And so, I gathered all of the old family photographs, and attempted to compose a story that chronicled my mother's life.

In one black-and-white photo, my mother appears to be in her mid-teens. She is pictured with her parents, her two sisters, and her brother. It looks as if they were at the beach, because they're in swimwear. My mother is smiling in this picture, and she looks happy and carefree.

A second black-and-white photo appears to have been taken a few years after the beach family photo. My mother is standing, and posing alone. It looks like a photograph taken by a professional, and I'm guessing that she's about 16 years old. Again, she's smiling.

In another photo, my mother is pictured with her mother and her two sisters. It's a beautiful picture of the women in the family, and it's interesting to note the strong resemblance between my mother and my grandmother. In this photo, my mother is probably in her late teens, and everyone is smiling.

I don't have any other photos of my mother from when she was still single. The next photo shows her on her wedding day. She looks stunning, dressed in a beautiful gown with a long flowing train. My father looks dapper in his tuxedo. My mother's sister and brother, my Aunt Teri and my Uncle Sal, are the matron of honor and the best man. Everyone in the photograph seems happy.

And then, the mood in the photos begins to change...

In the next dated photograph, my parents have been married about six years. She is 26 years old, and my father is 31. They're both seated at a table with another couple, Dora and Chris, in a nightclub setting. What stands out most is that their friends are smiling, but my parents aren't. Her smile is gone, and my father doesn't look happy either.

Another photo was probably taken at a family member's wedding. Most of my family, including my grandfather, and two cousins, are in the picture. Everyone is smiling, except for my mother. What was she thinking? If you could put words to the look on her face, they would possibly be, "What the hell am I doing here?" I really don't want to be here!" She isn't even looking at the photographer.

I'm struck by a couple of other photos. In one photograph, it's my first birthday. I'm sitting on my mother's lap in front of a birthday cake. Obviously, it's a happy occasion. I'm smiling, but she isn't. In fact, in this picture, she's only 31 years old, and yet, she looks weathered and troubled.

As the photographs move forward in time, and transition from black-and-white to color, one thing remains the same: in every photo taken after my mother was married, she never really smiles. It's so obvious and telling.

It's also interesting to note that there are no photographs of my father from when he was a child. Absolutely none. The first photograph I have of my father, was taken on his wedding day. This is sad, and it speaks volumes in a loud voice, to the type of people his parents were.

As mentioned at the beginning of this chapter, it's possible to chronicle someone's life, and the shifts in their emotions and feelings, simply by looking at a lifetime of their photographs. Most people will smile for a photograph, regardless of how they feel. She didn't. She couldn't bring herself to smile, even for the few seconds that it took to take a photo.

If you want to understand a person, look at their life, especially their past. My mother had a life. I don't think that she just woke up one day and become the person that I remember as an angry, unhappy, abusive mother. Rather, I imagine that her life experiences might have gradually brought her there. I don't know what her childhood was like. I only know that after she was married, she never smiled in a photo again. Was she ever really happy? Did she lose her capacity to feel joyful after marriage? And, if so, I wonder if this was why she didn't want anyone else to be happy either.

Chapter 12
A Visit from the Loan Sharks

❧

Y MOTHER WAS VISITED by two repres-
entatives of the mafia when I was about eight
years old, and again, after my father died,
when I was a teenager. The first visit concerned money that
my father borrowed from the loan sharks, and the second visit
occurred when my mother placed our house on the market. The
second visit will be shared elsewhere in this book.

During the first visit, two well-dressed men, wearing dark,
three-piece suits, paid an unexpected visit to my mother. It
was a hot summer day, on a Saturday afternoon. She was alone,
because my father was at work. There was a knock at the door,
and one of the men asked if they could come in and speak with
her. I was hiding on the staircase, eavesdropping.

One of the men politely said to my mother, "Mrs. R., I don't
know if you know this, but Jimmy owes us a lot of money, and he
hasn't been paying us back. It would really be a shame if there was
an accident, and something terrible happened to him, or to you
or your kids. We don't want to see that. We just want our money."

My mother appeared confused and frightened. She
responded: "I don't understand. I don't know anything about
this. What are you saying? Jimmy borrowed money from you?"
Her voice began to elevate in pitch, and crack a little.

The taller, older man seemed annoyed, and repeated, "I just
told you. He borrowed money from us, and hasn't been paying
us back."

After a brief pause, she asked, "How much?"

He responded, "Including interest, about $3000." (Today, this would be equivalent to about $30,000.)

Upon hearing this amount, my mother seemed stunned, and suddenly all of the color began to drain from her face, and her complexion turned pasty white. She sat down at the dining room table, while the two men remained standing. When I saw her reaction, I became frightened.

There was a brief pause, and then she said, "I don't understand. Why would he borrow money from you?"

The younger man responded, "He's a gambler. He keeps making bets with the bookies, and he keeps losing."

In disbelief, my mother repeated the word, "Gambler?" Then, after another pause, as she said, "Okay. If he owed you money, why'd you keep lending him more money, when he wasn't paying you back?"

The older man responded, irritated, and raising his voice a bit, "That's not the point. He's a big boy, okay! He knows the deal. He *owes* us the money! Why don't you ask *him* why?"

As my mother attempted to compose herself, she sighed, then responded: "I need to talk to Jimmy when he gets home. We'll try to figure out how to pay you. Is that okay?"

The younger man said, "Sure. We'll be back in a few days."

They left, and my mother sat there for a few minutes. I'm sure she was blindsided, since she had no idea of my fathers troubles. Then she got up, and poured and drank a glass of water, as she tried to gather her thoughts.

She took a deep breath. Then, my mother phoned my Aunt Teri, and, in a quivering voice, said: "Teri, Jimmy's in a lot of trouble. The mafioso was just here. Can you come over?"

My aunt and uncle arrived at our house quickly, and my uncle asked: "What happened? Is Jimmy home? Is he okay?"

My mother said that he was at work. Then she burst into tears, explaining, "I don't know what I'm gonna do. Jimmy's gambling. He borrowed a lot of money from loan sharks. I don't know how we're gonna pay them... Goddammit! Why the hell would he do this?!"

My Uncle Mike said, "Jesus Christ! I don't get it. Jimmy knows better." Then he paused

before adding, "Don't worry Vinni, we can lend you the money. If you want, I'll talk to

Jimmy when he gets home."

My mother nodded. My aunt hugged my mother, and said, "Do you want us to stay with you, or do you want to call us when he gets home?"

My mother said, "I'll call you when he gets home." Then they left.

When my father came home from work, I heard bits and pieces of the conversation.

"God damn it, Jimmy, how could you do this?! What the hell were you thinking?! They threatened me,"she shouted, through gasping and tears.

My father sounded as if he was crying too, saying, "I'm so sorry. I thought I'd win. Then I would've paid them, and had some extra money. I work and work, and I don't have shit."

She responded, her voice increasing in volume, "Win? Nobody wins! You don't have shit?! You have a house and a family. You're never happy with what you have. What the hell do you want? Look at the mess we're in now, Jimmy. Now you cry and say you're sorry. What good does that do?" I heard the both of them weeping.

There was a long pause, and then my mother said, "Teri and Mike said they'll lend us the money."

My father responded, "Shit. I don't like owing that guy."

My mother raised her voice again, "What do you wanna do?! We don't have the money. We have no choice."

After a few moments of dead silence, my mother phoned my aunt, her voice quivering, as she said, "Hello Teri, Jimmy's home. Can you come over?" I didn't hear the conversation that ensued, but, from what I understand, they got together, and worked out an arrangement where my parents borrowed the money from them, and would repay them in installments.

When the loan sharks returned, my Uncle Mike was at our house, and my father was at work. My uncle gave them the money, and he told them, "I'm paying all off Jimmy's debt. Now don't lend him any more money."

One of the men replied, in agreement, "That's fine. Look, we don't need this hassle. We're businessmen. Jimmy knew the deal. We just want our money."

My uncle replied, "Well now you got it." Then the two men left.

After this, there were big changes in my house. My mother had to go back to work in a blouse factory – a sweatshop, to assist in repaying this debt to my aunt and uncle, and she took complete charge of the finances, and paying the bills. My father gave his salary to my mother, and she gave him a weekly allowance.

My father never gambled again. However, his gambling stint created overwhelming

financial and emotional burdens in our family, and my mother never trusted him again.

She always resented the fact that she was forced to go back to work because of his actions. Often, she would tell him, "It's all your fault that I have to work in that shit-hole." He never responded. What could he say? She was right. It was his fault.

When I think about this situation, I wonder about my father's state of mind, and why he would do something like this, when it was common knowledge that it was dangerous to borrow money from loan sharks. They were connected to the Mafia, they charged high interest, and would harm you if you didn't repay them.

I know he was envious of those who were more affluent. Perhaps this was a contributing factor. Regardless of his motivations, this behavior was selfish. He only thought about what he wanted, and not about how this might endanger our family.

I wonder what would've happened if my father didn't get the money to repay the loan sharks? I'm pretty sure that he would've been assaulted, or worse. And they also threatened my mother. Further, it always bothered my parents that they were indebted to my aunt and uncle.

My father's debacle escalated the tension in their already strained relationship. Consequently, my mother's anger grew, and the arguments between my parents became more frequent.

Chapter 13
Resentments & Feuds

Y MOTHER'S SISTER, TERI, and her husband Mike, lived across the street. My uncle was about 5'7", bald, and usually wore a fedora. He liked to sing and whistle, especially crooner tunes. My aunt was around 5'5", she had reddish brown hair, and she was an attractive woman, with a warm and pleasant personality. She was always kind to me, and I considered her my favorite aunt.

My parents had unresolved resentments toward the both of them. First, there was jealousy, because my aunt and uncle appeared well off, without the financial struggles that my parents had. My aunt had a well-paying, white-collar job in an office, with good benefits, and a pension. My uncle had his own taxi business, which, according to my parents, was lucrative. They also lived in my grandfather's house, so their rent was minuscule.

In contrast, my parents had blue-collar jobs. Although my mother had a high school education, she lacked office skills, and couldn't find office work, so she was forced to worked in a sweatshop, with no air conditioning. She did piecework as a seamstress, which meant there was no hourly wage or benefits. Rather, she was paid according to how many blouses she sewed, and didn't know how much money she would make from one day to the next. Given her intelligence, I'm sure this wasn't the life she had envisioned.

Her anger at being forced to go back to work to repay the money my father borrowed, was intense. She was furious with my father for putting her in this position, and ashamed because she was indebted to my aunt and uncle. Since she had been an angry woman before, this certainly didn't help.

My father was a baker, and he didn't make a lot of money. He worked six days a week, and ten to twelve hours a day. He also had a second job on Sundays, where he mixed bread dough for a different bakery. His work environment had several hot ovens, and no air conditioning or ventilation.

My father began to work when he was nine years old, so he only had a fourth grade education. Yet, he read quite well, and quite frequently. He was also mechanically inclined, and talented at repairing things, which made him popular in the neighborhood. Nonetheless, the issue was about financial disparity. Given the contrast between the occupations of my parents and my aunt and uncle, jealousy festered.

Originally, we lived in the same house as my aunt and uncle, on the top floor. This house belonged to my grandparents, which my grandfather still lived in and owned. At some point, my Aunt Teri got married, so my grandfather moved to the basement apartment, and she and Uncle Mike moved into the first-floor apartment. Then, when my mother and father were married, they moved into the second-floor apartment. My Aunt Rita and Uncle Sal owned their own houses, and lived nearby.

When my Aunt Rita's husband passed away, she had to sell her house for financial reasons. Then, from what I was told, my parents were pressured into vacating their apartment, so my aunt could move there with her children. My parents weren't happy about this. Since they were presented with few options, they decided to purchase the house across the street. However, this move left them with ongoing financial problems.

When he passed away, my grandfather's estate and his final

wishes created even more tension between my mother and her sister. Since my grandfather didn't have a written last will & testament, he told my mother, my aunts and my uncle: "I don't need a will with the lawyers. I trust Teri, who has my money."

Then he told my Aunt Teri: "When I die, just share my money with your sisters and your brother." The total amount in my grandfather's estate was $8,000, so each adult child should have been entitled to receive $2,000. That didn't happen. (By today's standards, my mother's part of the inheritance would have been about $20,000.)

Often when money is involved, greed rears it's ugly head. Money usually brings out the worst in people, and this is what happened. My grandfather's wishes were not honored, and my mother was outraged. I'm guessing that my aunt felt that since she lent my mother the money to repay the loan sharks, even though this loan was repaid, she didn't have to give my mother her share of the inheritance.

Since my Aunt Rita was a nurse, and my uncle Sal was an architect, both of them were even more financially well off than my Aunt Teri and my Uncle Mike. So, when my grandfather died, they told my Aunt Teri that she could keep their share of the inheritance. They felt that, since she had assumed the burden of taking care of my grandfather, she was entitled to this money. My mother felt differently.

Nonetheless, my aunt refused to give my mother her share. My mother was livid! She considered this a major insult, and a slap in the face. Besides this, she felt that, upon my grandfather's death, my aunt and uncle now owned my grandfather's house, free and clear, and they had no intention of sharing the profits with their other siblings, if or when they sold this house. (Eventually, this is what happened.) Despite this, my Aunt Rita and Uncle Sal sided with my Aunt Teri, telling my mother, "Let Teri keep the money. She took care of papa."

This further angered my mother, and she told them, "Mind your own business. I want my inheritance. Papa left it to me. If you don't want your money, that's your business." She felt that they should've refrained from taking sides, especially if they weren't going to take hers.

I know that there were several arguments between my mother and my aunt, but to no avail. My mother never received her inheritance, and for years, my mother's battle cry was, "My sister stole my $2,000!"

This type of situation might've been a deal breaker in many families, and could have easily lead to permanent estrangement. This didn't happen. I think that bonds in Italian families are so strong, that estrangement is taboo and unthinkable. My mother didn't walk away from the relationship with her sister. However, she never forgave, never forgot, and never stopped complaining about this.

Chapter 14
Dinner and Boxing Gloves

⟨≈⟩

"I HATE PAPER DISHES," I thought to myself, as I set the table. We were only four people, and I never understood why we couldn't use regular plates. Yet, day after day, we were told to set the table with thin, white paper plates, stacked in twos, to support our dinners. Nonetheless, the food would leak through, and we would usually eat some paper along with our meal.

"Mom, why can't we just use regular dishes?," I asked.

"Just use two instead of one," she answered, annoyed, and shooing me away. I sighed, frustrated, because she really didn't respond to my question, but rather, offered what I saw as a ridiculous solution. We were already using two dishes, and it didn't help. But she didn't like questions, and definitely didn't like to be confronted or challenged.

If my sister and I asked too many questions, she would get annoyed, and spew the cliché: "Children should be seen and not heard." This really meant be quiet, and *stop bothering me with questions*. If she didn't like the particular question, she wouldn't respond, or simply say, "Leave me a-lone." (There was always an emphasis on the "a" in "alone.")

We owned a two-family house, and there were tenants on the second-floor, Jack and Italia. Our apartment was on the first floor, but we didn't spend much time there. Instead, we ate, and spent most of our time in the finished basement, even though our apartment was fully furnished, and had a living room, a huge eat-in kitchen, three bedrooms, and a full bath.

The basement was a large room, about 15 feet in length. Upon entering from the front door, on the right, there was a large white refrigerator, a gas stove and oven, and a sink. Our large dining room set was in the middle of the room. To the left, there was a China closet. Behind the China closet, there was a stairway which led to our first-floor apartment. Toward the front of the room, on the left side, there was a small bathroom that had a toilet, a tiny sink, and a shower.

At the back of the room, near the kitchen sink, there was a brown accordion door that led to an unfinished portion of the basement. That area had another large room that housed the furnace, and a workshop with my father's tools.

There was no television set in our living room upstairs; just a red, floral patterned sofa, a matching large cushioned chair, and a fake fireplace. Instead, we had a TV set in the basement, near the front entrance. My father would move an uncomfortable dining room chair, and face it towards the TV, so he could watch it. He preferred this to going upstairs and watching television on a comfortable sofa. One time, our television broke, so my father bought another TV set, and placed it on top of the broken set, rather than removing it and replacing it.

Thinking back, I have no idea why we lived in the basement, rather than the furnished three bedroom apartment, fully equipped with a large, modern kitchen, furnished with a white formica table with silver chrome legs, and four red and white chairs. My mother never cooked in that kitchen, and she never spent time in that living room. My parents only went into this apartment to bathe, or when it was time to go to sleep.

Although the basement was the designated family room, I tried to spend as much time as possible in the upstairs apartment, away from the rest of the family, and the constant accompanying din. I would sit in the kitchen alone, and play my guitar, read a book, or write poems or songs. Often, in the distance, I could hear the muffled sound of bickering coming from the basement. This was the norm.

My mother always sat toward the back of the room, at the head of table. It seemed like she was glued to this particular chair, adamantly unwilling to abdicate her throne. When she got up, no one dared to sit in her chair. It was *her* spot.

She always had a pack of Newport menthol cigarettes and a glass ashtray on the table, right in front of her. No one was allowed to touch her cigarettes. My mother smoked constantly, three packs a day, even while we were eating dinner. It wasn't unusual to have ashes in our food.

One night, close to six o'clock, the aromas of food, stale smoke, and a freshly lit cigarette filled the air. As usual, I felt hungry and apprehensive. *"I hope she doesn't start anything tonight,"* I thought to myself. And yet, I knew that she would behave exactly as she behaved every single night, when we assembled for dinner. I often wondered if she looked forward to this time of the day.

Minutes after sitting down, before anyone took their first bite, the bickering started, and my stomach did it's daily dance, beginning to churn with anticipatory anxiety. I wanted to hide, but I was hungry. I thought, *"Damn it. I hate this time of the day!"* And I wondered, *"Do other families bicker during supper?"*

Within minutes, my mother started to nitpick. Like always, she addressed me first: "Nell, why can't you fix yourself up more and put on more makeup, like your sister?" I didn't respond. She continued, now directing her next question in my sister's direction, "What do you think, Stella?"

My sister hesitated, and then responded, "Um, yeah, I agree

with you, mom."

The fuse was lit, and the arguments began. At that age, I didn't understand the difficult position Stella was stuck in, caught between my mother and me. If she didn't agree with my mother, then she would be the target of my mother's anger. This was the only way she knew how to protect herself.

Since I was too afraid to stand up to my mother, I misdirected my anger, and argued with my sister: "Mind your own business, Stella." I began to raise my voice, "You think you're better than me?" In reality, the person who hurt me – and who I wanted to hurt back – was my mother. But I feared her.

As my sister and I argued, my mother interjected, "Stop bickering girls, we're supposed to be eating dinner." Although she ignited the fire, time after time, she pretended that she had nothing to do with it, and blamed us for disrupting her meal.

My mother had mental health issues and was toxic, but she was also intelligent. She was brilliant at redirecting drama, so that we would fight with one another, and forget that she started the disruption. I think that she got an adrenaline rush from starting conflicts, because my mother absolutely loved the chaos.

Sometimes, she disguised her instigating in the form of a joke. "You better watch out, Nell, Stella has all the looks, and she might steal your boyfriend. But that's okay, you still have all the brains." Or, "Nell, why can't you get more friends, like Stella?" I can't recall any comments where my mother suggested that my sister should be more like me in any way, except, perhaps, in implying that I had "all the brains."

My sister wasn't completely exempt from criticism. She was just less of a target, because she was more compliant, and never dared to challenge my mother. Rather, she tried to mirror my mother, and keep a low profile.

For some unknown reason, my mother was obsessed with and hated, in her words, the "mousy brown" color of my sister's hair. When she was only 12, under my mother's direction, my sister was already lightening her hair with hydrogen peroxide, and later, coloring it.

(Decades later, I was at my sister's house, and she commented that her own daughter also had mousy brown hair, and she was encouraging her to color it too. I found it sad that history was repeating itself, and my niece was subjected to the same shaming that my mother imposed upon my sister.)

During some of these dinner explosions, my father avoided eye contact with all of us, unless, of course, he happened to be the target that day. If he managed to escape my mother's attention, he stared at his plate and continued eating, as if nothing was happening. But he too had his moments. He and my mother were constantly bickering. Sometimes, when they didn't want us to know what they were saying, they spoke in Italian.

I believe that there was a euphoric component that added to my mother's enjoyment of disruption. She was only happy when she was able to upset other people, and she continued to use this sadistic tactic to antagonize me throughout my life. No matter how many times it happened, instead of recognizing this, I fell right into her trap again and again.

Years later, I wrote this poem to document my feelings about dinner time:

Dinner time, the worst time of the day,
Seated both in silence and dismay...
As mom cracks the whip on her command,
We all crumble, so afraid to take a stand.

She engages in her usual berating,
And deep within, I feel my anguish grating.

My stomach churns, my appetite gone,
As her caustic words go on and on and on...

Cigarette ashes seasoning the food,
And acid burns with every bite I've chewed.
Passing the salt along with the toxic words,
As her venomous words relentlessly flow and spew.
I feel trapped at the table, terrified with fear,

Trying to hold back a gigantic flood of tears.
Her intimidating presence, cold and suffocating,

Attacking us all with endless deprecating.
Forced to leave all my thoughts unspoken,
while it feels like I'm drinking venomous potions,
and chewing glass that's broken.

Each meal was an endless walk through hell.
I recall the memories
of a frightened, helpless child,
And the sorcerer – my mother,
who, daily cast her spell.

Chapter 15
Incest & Molestation

N MY OTHER BOOKS, I briefly spoke about being sexually molested. At that time, I felt uncomfortable identifying the perpetrator, and sharing some of the more personal and upsetting details. However, I've grown since then, and I'm more comfortable with filling in some of the blanks.

I'm writing this chapter in the hope that, if you were molested or sexually assaulted, my experiences and insights might help you see that you're not alone, and you too can heal from, and transcend some of the pain you've experienced because of sexual assault.

I was ten years old, and my sister was seven and a half years old, when the molestation began, and it continued for a couple of years. According to the snippets I recall, during the quiet moments of the night, when we were sleeping, my father would come into our bedroom and molest us. Other times, since my father worked nights, and my mother worked during the day, he would inappropriately touch us while the sun was still in the sky. I don't know if, or how long, he continued to molest my sister, after he stopped molesting me.

At times, there was a song playing during the molestation. Years later, whenever I heard this song, I would have a panic attack, a result of my PTSD. I also cringed at, and was repulsed by the the smell of bread and yeast, because I associated this aroma with my baker father.

It's sad that I've associated music with my traumatic experiences. I am a musician, and music has always brought joy into my life. But, to this day, when I hear that song, it still sends a lightning bolt of anxiety throughout my body. Fortunately, mindfulness exercises have helped me to get past this trigger quickly.

During this period, the trauma of being molested was reflected in my school grades, which plummeted. I failed every subject, and consequently, I was left back, and had to repeat the fifth grade. This experience just piled on to the existing distress in my life. I believe that if I hadn't been sexually violated, I would have continued to excel in school.

I don't understand why the teachers never showed any concern regarding the dramatic shift in my performance. The year before, I had excellent grades, and I passed every subject. Obviously something was going on in my home life to make my grades deteriorate so suddenly. Didn't they wonder what was happening? Also, why didn't my mother notice that I was doing poorly in school? Every quarter, she looked at my report card, and she had to sign it.

Being left back was humiliating. My classmates knew that while they were moving forward to the sixth grade, I was repeating the fifth grade. Back then, there was an even larger stigma attached to being left back. Furthermore, all of the children that I'd spent the previous five years with, were no longer in a classroom with me, and I was surrounded by children I didn't know. This just added to my trauma and low self-esteem. I felt utterly defeated.

In my ten-year-old mind, it felt as if every time my former classmates looked at me, they assumed that I was stupid, because I was left back. I continued to believe this for a long time, until, when I was in my 30's, I returned to college, and earned and maintained a 3.9 grade point average. It was only then that I was able to see, much to my own surprise, that I was intelligent.

I can still remember the day when the nun, my teacher, asked me to step into the hallway, and softly said: "Nella, I'm sorry, but you need to repeat the grade." I did not look at her, and I didn't respond to her.

After a brief pause, she said: "Do you understand what I'm saying to you?" I nodded yes.

She continued, "Can you tell me what you're feeling?"

I said, "Nothing. I don't feel anything."

But I did feel something. I felt betrayed by my teachers. I wondered why they didn't help me. I felt betrayed by my father. Betrayed by my mother. I felt that I couldn't trust anyone to protect me.

I also felt that I had zero value as a human being. I believed that being left back was a punishment. I felt that God was punishing me because I let my father touch me, and I didn't stop him, and I didn't stop him from touching my sister. It was my job to protect my younger sister, and I failed to do so.

I also didn't understand why the nun was telling me this, rather than my parents. I wondered if she knew what my father was doing to me. I blamed myself. I told myself that all of this was my fault. But I was too afraid to share these thoughts with my teacher.

Being molested and being left back created a pivotal, life-changing moment for me. I expected that the worst would continue to happen to me. I felt and believed that I was completely worthless, and deserved nothing good in my life... and, in many ways, I lived up to those expectations.

Life went on and seemed to circle around me, as I continued to feel helplessly trapped in a tornado. I walked through the 10th, 11th, and 12th years of my life in a daze. I began to disconnect from my feelings, and I learned to dissociate as a means of self-protection, and emotional survival. There were many moments when I wished that I was dead. It felt as if each moment was a struggle, and I can't recall any joyful moments during this period.

I was molested again when I was 15 years old. I didn't date a lot, so I was naïve. I knew a guy named Carmine, who was a customer in the record store where I worked, and he seemed nice. He was attractive, with dark curly hair, and always wore a suit and tie. We went on a first date, we had dinner, a pleasant time, and he was a gentleman. So, we went on a second date. In the movie theater, Carmine put his arm around me, and seconds later, he suddenly put his hand into my blouse, and was fondling my breast. I'd never been touched like this on a date before, and I felt shocked and upset.

This experience also brought me back to flashbacks of being molested by my father, and the same feeling of being helpless. I whispered to him, "Stop. Please move your hand." He didn't respond, and didn't remove his hand. I pushed his hand away, got up, and angrily walked out of the theater, and home by myself.

Although this experience was traumatizing, I was more upset by the reactions of my parents. I walked in the door, began to cry, and told them what had happened. Instead of being sympathetic and consoling me, they didn't understand why I was so upset. They both laughed, thinking the situation funny, and felt that I was overreacting.

Then, a few days later, when Carmine called on the phone a few times, I refused to speak with him. Again, my parents couldn't understand why I didn't want to take his calls, and still did not understand why I was so upset. Not even a morsel of empathy.

It was traumatic to be molested, first by my father, and then, by a date, and these experiences had long, lasting effects.

I remember thinking to myself, "Why does this keep happening to me?"

I was less traumatized by being molested by Carmine, because he was out of my life, and no longer posed a threat. On the other hand, although the incest stopped by the time I reached my teens, I still had to live in the same house with my father. I was guarded, and afraid to be with him when we were alone, because I didn't know if this would happen again. My experiences led me to fear and distrust both parents due to my mother's physical and verbal abuse, and my father's sexual abuse.

The incest left me with severe PTSD, which included upsetting flashbacks, and uncomfortable body memories. I was easily startled, and afraid of the dark, so I slept with a night-light for decades. Years later, when I began to recall more repressed memories, and shared this with my therapist, she referred me to an incest survivors' group. I will always remember Pat, the group leader, who was also an incest survivor. She was a warm, nurturing woman, and she helped me a great deal.

In this group, I've met a lot of courageous women of all ages, and their love comforted and supported me. I was struck by the fact that, although some of these women were victims of incest many decades ago, they still felt the intense pain of this wound. I've learned that emotional scars remain. Eventually, I was able to look upon these scars as testimony to the fact that I was an empowered survivor.

With the help of counseling, I began to realize the full extent of what happened to me, and other parts of my life began to make sense. Counseling was difficult. I had to re-live the pain and the grief, and critically examine the many losses and struggles that this violation created. It took a long time before I was able to reach any level of forgiveness. Ultimately, I forgave for *myself*.

In hindsight, I can see that my relationship with my father was filled with contradictions. He protected me from my mother, but no one protected me from him. There were times when my mother tried to slap or hit me, and my father would intervene, grabbing her hand to stop her. When she berated me in his presence, he would tell her to stop.

I never asked my parents for anything, but one day I decided that I wanted to learn how to play the guitar. My mother was adamant about refusing this request. She would repeatedly tell me, "That's ridiculous. Girls don't play the guitar." My father felt differently, and he wanted to grant my request. My mother would argue with him, "We don't have money to waste on a guitar and an amplifier." (But we *did* have the money to get her hair done every single week.)

He argued with her, "What's the big deal? I think it's good that she wants to learn how to play an instrument." Eventually, he won this argument. He bought a guitar and an amplifier, and I was given weekly guitar lessons for about a year. To this day I still don't understand why my mother was so opposed to this.

As surprising as this might be, I have more unfinished business, and more lingering resentments toward my mother, than I ever had toward my father. Aside from the molestation, he didn't verbally and physically abuse me, as she did. He also died when I was a teenager, and I don't have many memories of him.

Nevertheless, I was deeply wounded by being molested by my father – someone that I was supposed to trust, and someone who was supposed to protect me rather than harm me. But the confusing thing is this: he always defended me and protected me from my mother. Although I've healed to a great extent, it took many years and a lot of hard work to get to this place. The journey is doable, but it is still arduous, and gut-wrenching.

Chapter 16

Tie-Dye and Love Beads

⚘

THE INCEST WAS BRIEF, but the emotional scars were deep and long lasting, and the verbal abuse by my mother continued. As a result of the sexual, physical and verbal abuse I endured from them, I distrusted both parents, and by extension, nearly everyone else, especially adults. Therefore, the rallying cry of the hippies, "Don't trust anyone over 30," spoke to me.

Although I connected with this slogan, and the idea of being a hippie, in reality, I was just a hippie *wannabe*. I wasn't interested in *free love*. Relationships were unimportant to me. I was also too afraid to experiment with drugs. However, I do have some fond memories of Boone's Farm Strawberry Hill and Apple wine.

Although I had no interest in the lifestyle, I loved the idea of being rebellious, and I especially loved the attire! I wore love beads, peace symbols, and tie-dye clothes. I dressed the part, but I didn't want to live it.

I also loved the fact that the hippies had an unapologetic, rebellious, fuck-you attitude. Like them, I was interested in anything that would upset my parents, and be a pain in their ass. This was my only way of fighting back, and it worked.

There were other reasons why I identified with hippies. I felt like an outcast, damaged and less-than in so many ways. I found myself out of sync with the rest of the world. Since I didn't fit in with my peers, and I feared that relationships included the possibility of being hurt and rejected, I avoided them. I convinced myself that I was proud to be a rebellious loner. Beneath this angry rebel, I was really lonely and afraid.

I hated the way my parents behaved: their abusiveness, their indifference, their selfishness, their ongoing battles, and how they were critical and envious of everyone around them. At the same time, I was financially dependent upon them, so I had nowhere to go. Since I felt imprisoned, I sought out ways where I could feel some semblance of autonomy.

During my early teenage years, I also became more vocal, and confronted my parents about the ongoing fighting and chaos in my family. Because I spoke out and challenged them, I became even more of a scapegoat. In their eyes, I was a troublemaker. They didn't like to be confronted, especially my mother.

In an exasperated tone, I would ask my mother, "Why are we constantly fighting in this house?"

Her response was always: "Come on, all families fight." I would say, "No. Not like this. Not every day."

And she would retort, "How do you know? You don't live in their house." My mother wanted to normalize behavior that wasn't normal, so these conversations were just frustrating and futile. Now, as I reflect back, I wonder what it was like growing up in my mother's house when she was a child, and if there was similar ongoing friction. Were there any similarities between our *normal* and her *normal* as a child?

Aside from the desperate need for autonomy, I was searching for an identity. Who did I want to be? The only thing that I knew for certain is that I didn't want to be anything like my parents. I also didn't want to be like my sister. While I was overtly expressing my frustrations, Stella retreated into denial. She was agreeable, and never protested or questioned our toxic environment. I guess this was how she learned to cope. I just couldn't follow her example.

Stella and I couldn't have been more different. She was outgoing, while I was shy. She was sociable, while I was more comfortable being a loner. We also had different interests. I played the guitar, wrote songs and poems, and I read books. She liked cheerleading and dancing, and had no interest in books, or playing an instrument.

However, we both acted out. We just rebelled in different ways. I embraced the hippie persona, and complained about the discord in our house, while she acted out in more covert ways. She got into trouble through high-risk behavior, which included poor choices of boyfriends. She was attracted to the *bad boys*.

One time, I was dragged into a dangerous and frightening situation that my sister created. The Police Athletic League (PAL) was a recreational club that recently opened in our area. The neighborhood kids would go there to listen to music, and play billiards and ping-pong. My sister heard about this place, and she wanted to go. I did not. But since, according to my parents, it was my job to "keep an eye of her," I was compelled to go with her, against my will and my better judgment.

We didn't know any of the kids that went there, and we were considered outsiders. My sister began to smile and flirt with some of the boys. When they reciprocated, their girlfriends became angry. Some of the girls began to argue with their boyfriends, saying: "Why are you looking at her?" or "I saw you flirting with her!"

Other girls directed their comments toward Stella: "Stop flirting with my boyfriend." Or, "Why are you looking at my boyfriend?"

These boys then re-directed their anger toward my sister. One of the boys called my sister a troublemaker. Before long, a few of the girls began to point at my sister, chanting:

"Troublemaker! Troublemaker!"

At this point, the two PAL counselors sensed that the situation was escalating, and they told us that we should leave, and offered to drive us home. They told the other kids that they were closing the club early, and it would be open tomorrow, which angered them even further. I think that they blamed my sister for this.

As we got into the car, a group of kids started shaking the car back-and-forth, trying to turn it over. The counselor who was driving the car, quickly drove away, and we were able to get home safely. However, it was a harrowing experience. I blamed my sister, and I felt it could've been prevented.

Aside from other differences between Stella and I, our taste in music greatly differed. While she was listening to Led Zeppelin and The Rolling Stones, I was listening to Bob Dylan, James Taylor, Judy Collins, John Denver, Simon & Garfunkel, and The Carpenters. I didn't like loud rock and roll, and preferred songs with meaningful lyrics.

I strongly identified with the song *I am a Rock*, by Simon & Garfunkel. For the first time, I felt that I wasn't alone. Every sentiment spoke to me: loneliness, fear, sadness, barriers, books and poetry... it was all there, mirroring my life.

In *Both Sides Now*, Judy Collins also reflected my sentiments, particularly: *"tears and fears,"* and, *"If you care, don't let them know."* Every day, I lived with hidden tears and fears that I was afraid to express, because it wasn't safe to do so. Finally, like Judy, I couldn't make sense of what life was about: *"It's life's illusions I recall. I really don't know life at all."*

In *Rocky Mountain High*, John Denver sung about leaving yesterday behind, and being born again. I desperately wanted to leave my yesterday behind, and experience some sort of a rebirth, somewhere else! Denver also sang about the beauty in nature, in the *"cathedral mountains,* or *"the serenity of a clear blue mountain lake."*

I pictured these beautiful images in my mind, even though they were far removed from my reality. I live in the Bronx, a city where houses were stacked on one another. I never saw a beautiful, blue lake, or a magnificent mountain, except in my own mind. However, I had a great imagination, and Denver's words helped me to redirect my thoughts beyond the limitations of my own surroundings.

In *Blowin' in the Wind*, Bob Dylan sang about unfairness, freedom, peace, and violence. These words spoke to me because there was a war going on in my own family, and there was no end in sight. And the answer was *in the wind*. I agreed with Dylan: if the answer did exist, it was certainly inaccessible.

In *Rhymes & Reasons*, Mary Travers expressed the feelings gnawing at my soul: *"So you speak to me of sadness and the coming of the winter. The fear that is within you now, it seems to never end. The dreams that have escaped you, and the hope that you've forgotten..."*

Sorrow, hopelessness, fear, and broken dreams were an integral part of my life. I felt as if I was lost in a dark forest, and there wasn't anyone who could take my hand and escort me out. Some of these songs gave me some comfort, because I knew that there were others who shared my feelings.

I kept searching for ways to rise above my circumstances and express myself. I was already writing poetry, and, as I mentioned earlier, I became interested in the guitar. I picked up the hobby after observing my cousin Phil, whom I deeply admired.

My guitar teacher, Mr. Gentile, was a sweet, soft-spoken man of Italian-American descent, probably in his 50's. He played in a wedding band, and gave guitar lessons on a part-time basis. Mr. Gentile was about 5'4", had a stocky physique, short, black hair, a little mustache, and eyeglasses, and he always wore a suit and tie. Once a week, Mr. Gentile came to my house to give me a guitar lesson for one hour. He played beautifully, and was a patient teacher.

I loved the guitar, and practiced diligently. After a while, I learned to play well, and I was so proud of this accomplishment. I would play my guitar in a secluded part of the house, away from the rest of the family. I was happy to spend my time alone, putting needed distance between myself and the never-ending noise that went on in my house. Since I was working in the music store at the time, I saved my money to buy another guitar that I fell in love with. It was a bright red, electric, hollow-body guitar, with a tremolo bar.

My music became my refuge, and brought about some emotional healing. My cousin Phil, the cousin I admired, who also played the guitar, eventually asked me to join him and my other cousin, Sal, who sang, to jam together. I really enjoyed this, and it meant a lot to me. I loved my cousin Phil. He was like a big brother to me, and I asked him to walk me down the aisle when I got married.

During my later high school years, I gradually moved away from the hippie persona, as I became more involved in school activities that I enjoyed. There were a few people who helped me transition into adulthood.

I was shy and somewhat of a loner, until I made friends with a classmate named Dawn, who was friendly, and upbeat. We both played the guitar at the school masses. "Why don't you join the guitar club?," she suggested.

I responded, "Well, I'm a little bit shy. I don't know if I would feel comfortable."

Dawn responded, "Don't be silly. You play so good. Look,

you're playing at masses... I'm in the guitar club. It's a lot of fun. We'll have a lot of fun." And so, Dawn convinced me to join.

Dawn was a good friend, and she helped me to become more outgoing and sociable. She was also responsible for introducing me to folk music, which I loved. In some ways, Dawn became the sister that I always wanted, but never had.

During my high school years, I also became close to two teachers, who were nuns. Their names were Sister Maura and Sister Mary. They were probably in their mid-20's, and they dressed in secular clothing.

Sister Maura was a soft-spoken, kind-hearted woman. She had long, wavy black hair, and she wore eyeglasses. Sister Mary also wore glasses, and she had short, dark hair. She had a great sense of humor. I got to know them, because they moderated the guitar club, and I remember thinking that they were very *cool*.

One day, I decided that I wanted to invite them for dinner, and my mother became defensive, automatically assuming that they were mother surrogates. She voiced her usual insecurities: "I don't understand why you're always looking for a mother," she would say. "You already have a mother." My mother was always threatened by other women in my life.

I never gave her any indication that these women were replacing her. However, I guess that, in some ways they were mother surrogates. To my mother's credit, even though she felt threatened by these women, they came to our house for dinner, and my mother was polite and hospitable to them.

Although we didn't keep in touch after I graduated from high school, in many ways, these two women gave me the motherly love that I lacked, and so desperately needed. I still think about them to this day, as I reminisce about their positive influence, and their kindness toward me.

Chapter 17
Death, Threats, and Other Losses

THERE WAS A PHONE CALL, and after hanging up the phone, my Aunt Teri paused for a moment, and then she began to cry. Through her tears, she said to my sister and me, "I'm sorry girls. Your father – just – died." It was Sunday, the 4th of July, and my sister and I were sitting in my aunt's living room. This day would never be the same again.

The last time I saw my father alive was a few days after my 17th birthday, around the 2nd week of June. I walked into his hospital room, and I remember showing him the red transistor radio that I received from my mother for my birthday. We were alone.

He said two words: "I'm sorry." Then he began to cry. This wasn't the first time that I saw him shed tears. In fact, he cried a lot. There were many times when the arguments between my parents brought him to tears, especially when my mother physically assaulted him. But this was different. These tears seem to be filled with fear and hopelessness – regret and remorse.

It was always frightening when I saw my father brought to tears – to lose control. Back then, it was unusual to see a man shedding tears. Men didn't cry. At least not in the presence of other people. Sometimes I would be upset and frightened when my father cried. There were other times when I became angry, because he was crying in response to my mother's physical assaults upon him. I saw him as weak and helpless. I had no respect for him. I felt like he should've defended himself.

On this particular day, I knew exactly why he was apologizing, and I didn't want to hear it. It was worthless to me, because it seemed disingenuous, a last-chance, deathbed apology, based on fear. At the same time, his words upset me. I suddenly realized the severity of the situation. He was going to die. He wasn't coming home. This revelation hit me like a lightning bolt, because I had no idea that this was a possibility. I didn't know what to say – what to feel. I just knew that I felt overwhelmed and I wanted to escape – so I ran out of the room... The next time I saw him, he was in a casket.

My father was in the hospital for several weeks prior to his death. Over the years, he has had other surgeries, primarily for stomach ulcers, so he was in the hospital several times. This time, what began as what was presumed to be a bleeding ulcer, became a mysterious illness that involved severe rectal bleeding of unknown origin.

For several weeks, his doctors had no idea what was happening. The surgeon did exploratory surgery, but still couldn't find the source of the bleeding. In the interim, he needed an incredible amount of blood transfusions. Since insurance didn't cover the transfusions, my cousin Angela rallied her coworkers to donate blood.

Eventually, the physicians concluded that he had an aortic aneurysm that couldn't be repaired. However, my mother suspected that the surgeon might have accidentally severed his aorta when he was performing surgery for the bleeding ulcer. Since the surgeon didn't charge my mother for these surgeries, this only reinforced her suspicions.

———————

I have snippets of my father's wake. He was prepared in a

sky blue shirt, a dark blue tie, and his iridescent blue suit – the only suit that he owned. He only wore this suit at weddings and funerals. Now he was wearing it to his own.

I remember a barrage of people from all over the neighborhood, who came to pay their

respects. There were hundreds of people lined up outside of Lucia Bros. Funeral Home, who shared tears, stories, and so many comments:

Jimmy was a saint.
What a shame.
Jimmy was a good man.
Oh my God, he was so young. Too young to die.
Whenever you needed help, Jimmy was always there.
Jimmy was a smart guy.
Jimmy was a sweet guy.
Jimmy was a lovable guy.
I loved the guy. I'm gonna miss him.
What a family man.
What a shame that his young kids won't have a father now.
His wife is such a young widow.

Other people shared stories of how my father helped them in some way:

I remember when my car battery died. I called Jimmy. He dropped whatever he was doing, and came to help me.

He always gave me a ride when I needed one.

Jimmy fixed my sink. I offered to pay him, and he said, "Don't insult me. I don't want any money. But I'll take a cup of coffee." Then he laughed.

They meant all of these compliments, and, in fact, my father was, in many ways, as they described. He was a complicated man. If you told any of these people that he was a child molester, you would have enraged them. They didn't see this side of my father, nor could they even fathom it. They also didn't see the depressed side of him. They just knew the easy-going, altruistic, upbeat Jimmy. A man who they all loved, and, at 52 years old, everyone agreed that he died too young.

My father was many things to many different people. Like everybody else, he had positive and negative qualities. But aside from my mother, my sister and I, no one knew the darker side of my father. And besides me, no one knew the remorse that he felt as he approached the end of his life. No one else heard the "I'm sorry." No one else could accept the apology he desperately wanted to offer, and when I heard it, neither could I.

———————————

Vinni, you have to pay the hospital bills. I work there. I don't wanna be embarrassed." My Aunt Rita was pressuring my mother, because she was concerned that she might be looked upon unfavorably, if my mother didn't pay our outstanding hospital bills.

"I don't have the money," my mother replied, almost pleading for some understanding. "Jimmy didn't have a pension. I'm getting very little Social Security money."

"Then you have to sell the house," my aunt coldly responded.

"Where are we going to go?" My mother sounded exasperated.

My aunt said, "You can live in Teri's house, in the apartment where Papa used to live. They said you can move there."

And so, much to my surprise, my selfish aunt successfully coerced my mother into putting our house on the market, against my mother's better judgment. My mother always regretted this decision.

If my Aunt Rita hadn't forced my mother to sell the house, to pay hospital bills, so *she* wouldn't be embarrassed, I believe we may have been able to remain there much longer, with the income we received from renting the other unit in the two-family structure. Besides, my father died under suspicious circumstances. These circumstances could've easily warranted an investigation, and possibly a malpractice lawsuit.

Eventually my mother sold our house at a great loss. To this day, I don't understand how she allowed her sister to bully her, when she was usually an aggressive, unyielding woman. I think that she was grieving, afraid, in a vulnerable state, so she wasn't thinking clearly. My aunt took advantage of this to keep up her appearances.

The period following my father's death was a stressful time filled with sorrow, fear, uncertainty, and many adjustments. We were forced to discard many of our personal possessions, including most of our furniture, since we were moving from a large, three-bedroom house into a small one-bedroom, three-room apartment.

Since we relocated to a different neighborhood, my sister and I had to commute to high school using public transportation. We had never travelled on buses before, and we were apprehensive. My mother also needed to commute, and she didn't drive. Eventually she worked out an agreement with a neighbor that allowed her to secure transportation.

As a young, 47-year-old widow, I'm sure my mother was shocked and distraught. My father unexpectedly died at the young age of 52, and she was now solely responsible for raising two teenage daughters, when we could barely make ends meet. She was in a precarious situation, and she must've been terrified about the future.

While our house was on the market, a situation occurred which showed desperation on my mother's part, and the loss of lucid thinking. One of our neighbors told my mother that the previous owners might have hidden money somewhere within the house. This didn't make sense, because we lived there for years, and we never heard this information before. Regardless, I think whoever told my mother this was just being cruel, considering the fact that my father had just died.

Nonetheless, this information catapulted my mother into a manic mode, and she became frantic in efforts to find this hidden money. She instructed my sister and I to look through all of the closets, and to search for hidden compartments where money might have been stashed.

When we were unable to find the elusive hidden money, she became agitated and unhinged, yelling at us because our attempts were unsuccessful: "Goddamnit! What good are you kids?" Consequently, her moods vacillated from livid to sobbing sad. She was desperate.

Then, a final nail in the coffin: the local mafia paid us another visit, to make selling the house even more difficult. Like before, two well-dressed, middle-aged men knocked at our door, and asked to speak with my mother.

One man said, "Hi Mrs. R. I'm so sorry about Jimmy's death. What a shame. He was a young man."

Guardedly, she said, "Thank you."

He continued, "Anyhow, we heard you wanna sell your house."

She responded, "Yes. That's right. Why?"

The man spoke again, "Well, we don't want the coloreds – the moulinyans, buying your house. We want to keep the neighborhood white."

My mother said, in a frustrated tone, "Look, I have to sell my house to pay my husband's medical bills. Now you're gonna tell me who I can sell my house to? Are you kidding me?"

He answered, "Do we look like we're kidding?" After a pause, he said, "Look, you're a young widow. You have young kids. We'd hate to hear your house accidentally caught fire. You already have enough problems, don't you?" He paused to let my mother absorb his words, then he said, "No moulinyans, capeesh?"

My mother sighed and nodded yes. After they left, she began to cry. Then she phoned my Aunt Teri, and told her what had happened. My Aunt Teri and Uncle Mike had already moved out of the neighborhood, but arrived at our house soon after.

My mother said, "I can't believe this. They're telling me I can't sell my house to colored people. *Che cazzo!* (What nerve!) What am I supposed to do if colored people wanna buy my house?" Her voice became louder as she continued, "They said – well, implied – they'd burn my house down! I didn't even wanna sell my house in the first place. Then Rita kept pressuring me! Oh my God!"

My aunt said, "Vinni, I know you're upset. It's gonna be okay."

Then my uncle took a puff of his cigar, and spoke: "Wait a minute. Didn't you say your tenant might wanna buy the house?"

My mother said, "Yeah. He said he was thinking about it. Why? Should I ask him again?"

My uncle responded, "I would. You got nothing to lose."

Eventually, our tenant, Jack, decided to buy our house, and my mother took a great loss, selling it for less than she paid. Since Jack couldn't get a mortgage for the full amount, my mother gave him a second loan for the balance. Every month, Jack sent my mother a check.

My mother never forgot about both of these visits and threats from the mafioso, and continued to speak about them for years to come, always with the same anger. I was present both times, and I never forgot about these visits and threats either.

Once we moved in, we were uncomfortable living in this tiny apartment. It was small, cold and damp, and after living in a large house, it felt like we were all crammed into a sardine can. The apartment had one bedroom, and my sister slept with my mother. I was tossed into the living room to sleep on an uncomfortable sofa-bed, and woke up every morning with back pain.

There were additional inconveniences as well. Unlike our other neighborhood, where all of the stores were within walking distance, the stores in Throggs Neck were far away, so we needed to drive to the supermarket, to the pharmacy, and to every store.

My mother hated this apartment, and resented my Aunt Rita for bullying her into moving. Often, she would look toward the heavens, and talk to my deceased father: "Why did you leave me, Jimmy? Look where I have to live now." Despite all of the issues I had with my mother, in terms of living in this apartment, I shared her sentiments.

Chapter 18
Tools and Barbie Dolls

AFTER MY FATHER'S DEATH, our family dynamics drastically changed, and we lost all of our of independence. Since my mother wasn't usually the type of woman who would willingly allow anyone to control her, I don't think she asked for, or wanted interference or help to this extent.

Nonetheless, while my mother was vulnerable and grieving, some family members, altruistic or otherwise, seized control. For example, my Uncle Sal assumed the paternal role, and looked upon himself as the new head of *our* house. Maybe he was trying to be helpful, but it certainly didn't feel that way.

The first thing he did was to take all of my father's expensive Craftsman tools, "You're not gonna use them," he asserted, "so I might as well take them. Anyhow, I'm sure Jimmy would've wanted me to have them."

My uncle's comment was absolutely false. My parents disliked him. My father would never have wanted him to receive any of his possessions. If my mother was in her right state-of-mind, and her usual aggressive self, she would've protested, because she knew how my father felt about my uncle.

My parents often spoke about and ridiculed him. "He acts like a big shot," my father would say.

My mother would chuckle and agree, "Please! He thinks he's hot shit."

Then they would both laugh hard.

But I guess my uncle had the last laugh, because he took all of my father's high-priced tools, and he didn't even have the courtesy to ask my mother's permission to do so. Rather, he seized them, and later offered my mother a feeble explanation.

The saddest part is, my father didn't have much, but these were his prized possessions. He loved, and was so proud of his tools, he enjoyed working with them, and worked hard to earn the money that purchased them.

Yet, just days after his burial, my uncle did a power grab, and my father's tools were already in his possession. I think he probably thought my mother would give them to someone else, and he wasn't going to let that happen.

If my father were alive, he'd probably say, "Damn it! That guy always had his eye on my tools." And he would have been right.

Back then, Craftsman made the most expensive tools money could buy; but my uncle was financially well-off, and could've bought his own Craftsman tools. Perhaps this was about greed and entitlement, or maybe he simply just wanted them.

As mentioned elsewhere in this book, my mother held grudges, and she never forgot about an injustice that was done to her. This included the way my uncle went about confiscating my father's tools. She felt that either my sister or I were the rightful heirs to my father's most prized possessions. So, a few years after my father's death, my mother decided to confront my uncle.

When she told me she was going to do this, all I could say was, "Well, good luck getting them back, mom."

My mother said that even if she didn't get back the tools, she was planning to, "confront that arrogant bastard, and aggravate the hell out of him." I laughed, because I knew that no one was more talented at this than she was.

According to my mother's version of their encounter, my

uncle made the big mistake of visiting with her, and having a cup of coffee.

"By the way," she said casually: "Can you give my daughter Jimmy's tools? She just bought a house, and they don't have any. It would really help them."

She said he seemed taken aback, and he replied in a surprised tone, "What? Umm. I don't know what happened to them. I don't even think I have them anymore. In fact, I think I might've thrown some of them away."

(My mother said, she thought to herself, "Yeah, right.")

She said, "Come on now. Even I know nobody throws away tools. Jimmy bought them

from Sears, and they were very expensive... But, okay then, if you threw some of them away, just give my daughter the ones you still have. Stuff like hammers, screwdrivers, wrenches. Stuff you wouldn't normally throw away." (Clearly, my mother wasn't going to let him play games with her.)

My uncle wasn't the type of guy who liked being confronted, and her comments seemed to upset and anger him. According to my mother, this is when he became agitated, and tossed his hands in the air, "God damn it! They can buy their own tools!"

My mother responded, raising her voice, "These tools *are not yours*! They were my husband's tools, and they belong to *my daughters!*"

"I don't know what to tell you," he said.

My mother said she was very angry at this point, and said, "Oh that's nice. You robbed my husband's tools, and never intended to return them. You're a thief! Get the hell out of here!" Then my uncle got up, and he left.

In telling me the story, she added, "Can you friggin believe this?" I believe my mother knew she would never get back any of the tools, but she wanted to confront and aggravate him. It worked.

_____

Shortly after my father's death, after taking his tools, the next thing my uncle Sal did was to acquire a huge dumpster. Then *he* decided what we could keep and what we needed to throw away. He didn't ask us what we thought, or for our permission to do so. Rather, his rationale was, "Listen. You can't fit all this junk in that tiny apartment. We gotta get rid of stuff." Actually, the items he threw away, and what he called "junk," were small, and would have "fit" into our new apartment. There was more than enough room for them.

It felt as if my uncle wanted to flex his muscles, in a cruel way, and at our expense. At the same time, this seemed so out of character for him. Nonetheless, this behavior was primarily targeted at my sister and me, who were just kids. We were only 15 and 17 years old at the time.

We were forced to discard personal items that were important to each of us. There were so many things that my sister and I had accumulated and cherished for years, and we considered them keepsakes.

We had already lost our father. We were losing the home where we lived. We were losing our friends. We were losing a neighborhood that was familiar to us. And, without a second thought, or an ounce of compassion, we were losing – being forced to lose most of our personal possessions, that were deeply important to us.

As my uncle coldly grabbed and tossed things that we cherished, each discarded item felt like an assault, as if we were losing a piece of our history, and a piece of ourselves. My sister and I had Barbie and Ken dolls that were housed in beautiful blue cases. We took care of them – loving care. Each doll had an extensive wardrobe, and it took years for us to save enough money to buy each piece of clothing. When we were younger, we would spend hours – years – enjoying and playing with these dolls. We wanted to keep them. Now, gone in a heartbeat!

I also had a stamp collection that was important to me. I would collect stamps, and it brought me a lot of joy to acquire them, and glue them in the appropriate places in the album. This brought me comfort, and sense of accomplishment and satisfaction. They too were tossed into the dumpster, because my uncle consider them "junk."

And then there was my baseball card collection, which I loved, and also took great pride in. It took years to collect all of them. In fact, I won many of them from other kids, and I was so proud of myself, and my talent for winning these cards. Although I no longer played with them, like my Barbie and Ken dolls, and my stamp collection, they were still important to me. I wanted to keep them. And again, within the flip of a wrist, my uncle threw them into the dumpster without a second thought.

Everything that was important to my sister and myself was being irreverently discarded, like worthless pieces of trash. Chunks of our lives and our memories were being thrown away without our consent. My uncle had daughters, and I doubt he would've flippantly thrown away their dolls or possessions that they considered to be valuable.

During this dark time, there were so many losses that we were grieving: the death of my father, the loss of our home and our friends, the loss of the familiarity and convenience of our neighborhood, and, of course, the loss of personal and precious possessions.

Chapter 19
Meeting Kenny

THERE ARE SOME MOMENTS IN LIFE that seem so insignificant at the time, yet, they can be life-changing. For me, working at the local record store, and eventually meeting Kenny, was one of those moments.

Casa del Disco was a local Italian and American record store in my neighborhood. The store primarily sold imported Italian 45's, albums, and cassettes, but they also sold American records. The record store had speakers blasting music so loud, that you could hear it as you walked by. Later, I learned that the owner purposely played his music at high volumes to bring attention to his store.

Each time I passed the store, I wondered what it would be like to work there, and play all of latest music on an awesome sound system. And so, one day I walked into the store and asked Mario, the owner, for a job. Mario was probably in his 30's. He was a nice looking man, about 5'6", had blue eyes, and a charming personality.

Mario was an educated man. When he lived in Italy, he was an architect. Unfortunately, when he came to America, he was unable to get the proper licenses to continue in his profession. Therefore, he became an entrepreneur, and started his own business –a record store. This small business became lucrative, primarily because of his likable personality, and his ability to befriend his customers.

"Hi Mario, I don't know if you remember me, but I buy my records here all the time," I said.

Mario responded, "Oh yeah, I remember you. How are you?"

"Oh, I'm pretty good. Thanks... Listen, I would love to work here. Would you be interested in giving me a job? I play the guitar and I love music."

He said, "Many of my customers are Italian. Can you speak the language?"

I knew that my Italian skills were limited, but I really wanted this job. So, I said, "Oh yeah. I can speak and understand some Italian. I'm taking the Italian language in high school, and my parents talk Italian."

He smiled, not quite believing me, and he said, "Well, you have a nice, friendly personality." I smiled, and thanked him. Then Mario said, "What days can you work?"

I answered, "I can work after school and on weekends." (It sounded as if he was going to hire me, and I began to get excited.)

Finally he said, "Okay. You're hired. You can start working here on Saturday. Be here at 9 o'clock. Then we can talk about the other days that you can work after school."

I said, "Great, thanks so much!" Then he told me what my hourly wage would be. Quite frankly, although earning my own money was appealing, I didn't care. I just knew I wanted to work there.

As I walked out the door, smiling, I thought to myself, *I can't believe that I got this job. Wow! I'm so excited!*

I went home and told my parents, and they approved. A few days later, I was at the store, promptly at 9am, and I began to work. Of all the jobs I've had in my life, second to counseling, this will always be the job that I loved the most. I worked after school, and on weekends, and I could listen to all of my favorite songs. I was thrilled to work there.

When the store wasn't busy, I swept the floors and dusted

all of the records, and when Mario stepped out, he left me in charge. He trusted me, and his trust in me was important. I was constantly busy, and I loved it. The store had air-conditioning (which I didn't have at home), a great sound system, and I was able to get away from the constant bickering in my house.

Mario was a wonderful person and terrific boss. He was witty, outgoing, and kind-hearted. More importantly, Mario was the first adult who treated me with respect, as an equal. He appreciated me, and made me feel valued.

Enzo and Kenny were customers who frequented Casa del Disco. They both had Beatle-type haircuts. Enzo was a short, stocky fellow, with a brash personality. He spoke in a loud voice, was melodramatic, and seemed needy for attention. Very few people annoyed my boss Mario, but Enzo got on his nerves.

In my teenage years, I was quiet and soft-spoken, and Enzo was definitely not my type.

Nonetheless, he asked me for a date once, "Hi Nella, do you have a boyfriend?"

I should have realized he was going to ask me for a date, but it just didn't occur to me, so I responded, "Umm. No."

Then he said, "Okay then. Would you like to go to dinner with me?"

I wasn't interested, and I said, "No, but thank you."

However, I was attracted to his friend, Kenny, who was his complete opposite. Kenny's personality was similar to mine. He was a quiet, soft-spoken guy, with a gentle manner. He was handsome, fairly tall, and had an olive complexion, and big brown, soulful eyes. I never understood how Kenny and Enzo were friends, except for the fact that they played in the same band together.

Kenny would come into the store a few times a week, asking,

"Can you please unlock this cabinet? I'd like to look at some of the cassette tapes." He would look at the songs on several tapes, but he never purchased any of them.

"Are you interested in buying any of them?" I would ask.

And the answer was always, "No thank you. Not today." We went through this ritual again and again.

When I ask Kenny today, he swears he purchased cassette tapes from me, but I don't remember that. In fact, Mario and I used to joke that Kenny would keep coming into the store, but never wanted to put his hand in his pocket, and spend some money. Mario would say, "Kenny's coming here to see you, Nella." And the feeling was mutual. I looked forward to seeing him too.

It's interesting how fate works. Although Kenny and I would exchange pleasantries whenever he came into the store, he never invited me on a date. Then, after my father died, and we relocated, I had to quit the job that I loved; I could very well have never seen Kenny again. However, my sister and I still went to dances in the neighborhood at Caiti Hall, and that's where I ran into Kenny again.

It was six months after my father's death, and coincidentally, Kenny's band was playing at this dance. Since I was interested in playing in a band too, I approached him.

He said, "I'm sorry about your father. Mario told me."

I responded: "Thank you. He passed away during the summer."

He asked, "Do you still live in the neighborhood?" I explained that my mother had to sell our house, we moved, and now I lived in my aunt's house in Throggs Neck, which was a few miles away. He said he lived rather close to me, about 3 miles away, on Bruckner Boulevard, near the Korvettes department store.

Although I was attracted to, and interested in Kenny, I wanted to play in a band even more. So, since that was my priority at the time, I asked, "I really want to play in a band. Do you know any bands that need a guitarist?"

He said, "Well, not right now. But if you want, I'd be happy to come over your house and show you the songs that we play, and we can play them together. What do you think?"

I loved the idea, and I responded, "That sounds cool." We exchanged phone numbers and addresses, and he asked if he could come the next evening. And he was there promptly, the next night, and many other nights.

Kenny would bring his guitar, and we would play songs together nearly every evening. I really liked him, and he seemed to like me too. We got to know each other, and eventually our friendship became a romantic relationship. We began to date, and we fell in love with one another.

Kenny was everything I wanted in a life partner. He was smart, funny, sensitive, kind, and respectful. We had so much in common, especially a love of music. His parents were nice, kind-hearted people too. On a beautiful Sunday in July, two and a half years after meeting Kenny, we were married.

My relationship with Kenny has changed my life in so many ways. We have a strong bond and ongoing love for one another. He's supported me through every struggle in my life, and we've also shared many joyful moments. Meeting and marrying Kenny was the best thing that ever happened to me, and I couldn't ask for a better life partner.

Chapter 20
Meltdowns and Knives

P RIOR TO MY FATHER'S DEATH, I saw a lot of erratic and violent behavior that my mother displayed. However, I never saw the full extent of her mental illness until a couple of years after he died. At the time, we were living in the first-floor apartment of my aunt's house.

The first unforgettable incident happened when my sister mentioned the possibility of getting her own apartment. The second incident was equally memorable, because the violence was directed toward me, when my mother threatened to kill me with a kitchen knife.

Regarding the first firestorm, my mother became enraged when my sister mentioned that she was thinking about moving out, and getting an apartment with one of her friends. (I think my mother was terrified to be alone.) Stella simply said, "My friend Susan and I were thinking about getting an apartment together."

My mother would often tell my sister and I, "The only way you're gonna leave this house is if you get married or you're dead." Therefore, it wasn't surprising that my sister's comment upset my mother. Still, her reaction was way over-the-top.

Suddenly, she rose from her chair, walked into the living room, got on the floor, and began to kick her feet, and twirl in circles. She resembled a child who was having a temper tantrum. Since she was a large, middle-aged woman, this whole scene looked bizarre. A few minutes later, she got off the floor, sat back in the chair, stared ahead, and appeared to be unresponsive and catatonic.

Since I was engaged at the time, and my fiancé was present, I was embarrassed and stunned. My sister tried to talk to her, "Mom, why are you doing this? Don't get so upset." My mother looked away, expressionless, and ignored my sister's comments.

Looking at me, Stella said, "Do you think she had a seizure?"

I responded, "I don't know. I don't think so. It looks like she doesn't know that we're here. That's not a seizure."

Stella attempted to talk to my mother again, "Mom. Mom, can you hear me?" There was no reaction or response, and my mother was still avoiding eye contact with all of us. I could see that Stella was starting to panic, and I could feel myself getting panicky too. My mother had a glassy-eyed, far-away look. It was frightening, and we didn't understand what was going on.

At this point, I told Stella I was going to call 911, but she said, "Wait. I'm gonna get Aunt Teri." I didn't think this was a good idea, because my family tends to panic easily. However, before I could respond, Stella darted out the door, and up the stairs, to summon my aunt.

In the meantime, I looked at my mother and said, "Mom, can you hear me?" She was still gazing away, and didn't knowledge me. I turned to Kenny, and said, "What do you think?"

He shook his head, and responded, "I have no idea."

Since my Aunt Rita was visiting my Aunt Teri at the time, she took it upon herself to come downstairs alone. Even though my Aunt Rita was a nurse, asking her for help was a bad idea, because she was abrasive, and had a talent for making a bad situation much worse.

My aunt entered our apartment, looked at my mother, and she seemed unsurprised. *Completely unphased.* I was holding the phone, and told her I was going to call 911. She yanked the phone out of my hand, slammed it down on the receiver, and yelled,

"That's ridiculous! No one is calling 911!"

She called my mother by name, "Vinni. Vinni." My mother didn't look at her or respond to her. It was as if my mother was in her own world, unaware of everyone around her. My mother suddenly began to break out into a sweat, so my aunt took a small dish towel, wet it, and patted my mother's head. Then she directed her comments toward my sister and myself, yelling: "This is all your fault! What did you kids do to her? She has a heart condition. Are you trying to give her a heart attack?!"

Kenny responded, "They didn't do anything to her. Stella just said she was thinking of moving out, and getting her own apartment."

My aunt completely ignored Kenny's comments, and said, "You kids upset her, and created all of this. Just leave her alone now. She's fine." Typical of my aunt, like a tornado, she swept in, created more havoc with her hostile words and presence, then she immediately exited.

A few minutes later, my mother seemed to return to *normal*, and I use the word "normal" loosely. She looked around the room, and suddenly seemed to be aware of the fact that we were sitting around the table. Then, she behaved as if nothing had happened, and said, "Why don't we have some coffee? Stella, make some coffee, and we'll have a piece of cake."

(My sister never talked about getting an apartment again.)

Later that evening, my fiancé turned to me and said: "What's wrong with your aunt?" He already knew that there was something wrong with my mother. If nothing else, he knew that she was a troublemaker, childish, and a vindictive, angry woman. But this episode was way over the top, and he thought my aunt's reaction was odd.

As I revisit this story, I realize something that previously escaped my attention. Why wasn't my aunt surprised? Why didn't she think my mother's behavior was bizarre? Why was she so sure that my mother didn't need medical attention, and she was "fine now?" Her reactions suggest that she might have seen this behavior before, and this is why she wasn't surprised.

As crazy this meltdown was, a few months later, there was another incident that made the previous occurrence seem insignificant in comparison. My mother became enraged by something I said. I don't recall what that was. However, I do remember that she suddenly positioned herself behind me, and grabbed a kitchen knife, pulled me close to her, pressed it against my throat, and said, "I dare you to say one more word. If you do, I swear to God, I'll slit your throat."

I was shocked and terrified. I didn't speak, because I truly believed she would kill me. After a few seconds, she released me from her grip, and no further words were spoken between us. I immediately phoned my fiancé, and told him what just happened. He asked me where I was now, and if I was safe. I said that I was. We spoke a bit more, but I was too shaken to continue the conversation for long.

I will never forget how quickly my mother became enraged to the point of violence, simply because she disliked my comment. To this day, I believe that if I spoke, she would have cut my throat. Yet, why was I so surprised? This wasn't her first act of violence. When I was five years old, she gave me a black eye and a swollen lip. Another time, and she shoved a bar of soap into my mouth. But this was different. Being a victim to her physical abuse as an adult has always bothered me.

Over the years, I've thought about this violent memory, yet, I never had the courage to speak to her about it. I've tried so hard to erase it from my mind, or deny that it even happened, although I have been thus far unsuccessful.

Since some of my mother's behavior was contradictory, at times, so were my feelings toward her. For example, during periods when we were estranged, my mother would send me *thinking of you* cards, where she wrote: "Out of sight, but never out of mind." Why? Was she trying to clear her conscience, and shift the blame to me? Was this gaslighting? Did she really miss me?

Once, after a two-year estrangement, she came to my home with a man I didn't know, and knocked on my door, because she wanted to reconcile. It was during the summer, on a Saturday. At the time, I had been married for a few years. When I opened the door, I was shocked. She was the last person that I expected to see. And as I looked at her, I was flooded with emotions. It was awkward and surreal.

I said, "Umm... Would you like to come in?"

She responded, "Okay. This is my friend George." She gestured to her companion. "Can he come in too?"

I said, "Of course. I'm not gonna leave him standing outside." She and George chuckled nervously, and so did I. She introduced him again, and George shook hands with my husband and me. Then my mother and Kenny exchanged awkward hellos.

She asked if I had an ashtray. Although we didn't smoke, we kept an ashtray for guests. I can't remember much about our conversation, but I still remember her cigarettes. Maybe because she was chain smoker, and cigarettes were such a huge part of our lives when we were growing up.

I noticed that she had changed brands. After two years of estrangement, and a few moments of awkward silence, the first thing I said was, "Oh, so you don't smoke Newport's anymore?"

And she responded, "No. I like Virginia Slims now. I heard they have less chemicals."

I said, "I guess that's good."

What else did we talk about? I think she said she missed me, and asked me if I missed her too. I believe I said that I did. We agreed to try again, and we reconciled. As I reflect, I wonder... did we really miss each other? Or, did I just miss the fantasy of who I wished she could be, and did she miss the fantasy of who she wanted me to be.

I wish I could close this chapter by saying we lived happily ever after, but that didn't happen. Instead, we repeated the same dance. Gradually, the same patterns began to emerge again. She went back to criticizing me, and I went back to feeling hurt, and walking away from the relationship. And then, after a time we would reconcile again and again. Nothing really changed.

Periodically, I thought about the night when she held a knife to my throat, and I just couldn't understand why she wanted to reconcile with me, when there was a strong possibility that she really hated me, and wanted to kill me.

Decades later, when my mother disinherited me, this memory re-surfaced, and reinforced the fact that I was right. She really did hate me, and again, given how she really felt about me, I will never understand why she wanted to reconcile with me.

Chapter 21
Adopted

ONE OF MY MOTHER'S FAVORITE SAYINGS was "lies have short legs," because she said that eventually the truth would always reveal itself. However, she didn't follow her own advice, because she was hiding an enormous and life-changing lie.

I lived the first 39 years of my life believing that I had my father's dimples, my maternal grandmother's smile, my grandfather's eyes, and my mother's light skin complexion. This information is documented in my pink baby book, and it was vocally reinforced throughout my youth. This was my reality. Every time I went to a doctor's appointment, I gave them my mother and father's medical history – a history that was fabricated, and based upon lies.

Then, one day, by accident, I accidentally discovered that I was adopted. In a split second, I realized that everything I thought I knew about myself was a lie. It was one of the most shocking moments in my life.

Sometimes I'm sorry that I discovered the truth, because it was so traumatizing. At the same time, I think it was meant to be, because I believe that everything happens for a reason. On the plus side, this knowledge freed me from the lifelong fear that I shared DNA with my parents, who I considered to be mentally ill.

It was a beautiful, sunny, July day, and I was excited because my husband and I were going on vacation to Cancun. Since this would be my first time traveling out of the United States, and on an airplane; I needed either a passport, a birth certificate, or a baptismal certificate. Since I was rushed for time, and couldn't find my birth certificate, I decided to get a copy of my baptismal certificate.

It was a short drive from my office to Our Lady of Mount Carmel church, where I was baptized. Since their files weren't computerized at the time, the receptionist was able to retrieve the original baptismal certificate. As she glanced at it, and assuming I already knew, she innocently said, "Oh, so you were adopted." It was just a rhetorical statement – a polite attempt at small talk.

After hearing her words, since I didn't want her to know that I had no idea I was adopted, I smiled and responded, "Yes, I was." Internally, I felt as if I had been hit by a truck. I felt my body begin to tremble. I began to feel nauseated, and my heart began to pound like a loud bass drum, but I tried to appear calm.

Then she gave me a copy of my baptismal certificate, and began to explain how the information was arranged. My current first name was on the first line, but there was another name in parentheses — Elinore. She commented that this name was taken from my original birth certificate, and was given to me by my biological mother, before it was changed by my adoptive parents.

I thought to myself: *My name was changed? What?!*

The next two lines had the names of my (adoptive) parents. Following my mother's name (in parentheses) was the first and the last name of another woman — a name I didn't recognize. She said that this was the name of my biological mother.

My thoughts began to race, and I became overwhelmed by the reality that an unknown woman gave birth to me. My queasiness increased, so I gave her a check for the fee, thanked her, and quickly exited.

As I stood outside of the church, I glanced at the baptismal certificate again. I tried to remain calm and compose myself, but that was impossible. As I looked at the document, I kept hoping that I misread it, but there it was in black-and-white. I got into my car, and my whole body began to shake.

My thoughts began to race: *What the hell! I'm adopted?! I can't believe this! I lived all of these years and never knew? Did my cousins know? Oh my God! Did my sister know?! Why the hell wasn't I told? I can't believe this! I'm not even Italian?!*

As I drove home, my hands were shaking, my body continued to tremble uncontrollably, and I struggled to steer the car. As I walked in the door, I immediately phoned my husband, who was still at work. "Honey, you're not gonna believe this. I just got my baptism certificate, and I found out I'm adopted." My voice got louder, and higher in pitch, "Can you freaking believe this?"

He was supportive, and said: "Try to stay calm. I'm on my way home. We'll talk about this when I get there. Remember, you always had a feeling you were adopted. Just don't call your mother until we talk about this."

After hanging up the phone, I reflected to when I was ten years old, and I asked my parents if I was adopted. At that time, I felt unwanted and unconnected from the rest of the family, I was being sexually, verbally, and physically abused, all of my grades plummeted, and I had to repeat the fifth grade.

I remember bits and pieces of that conversation. Both of my parents were sitting at the kitchen table at the time. I asked both of them: "Am I adopted?" They both froze, and they appeared to be startled.

My father quickly said, "No."

My mother said, "Why are you asking that? What gave you that idea?"

Then my father said, "Did someone tell you that?"

I was ten years old, and I had no idea why they were

bombarding me with so many questions. I said, "I don't know why I'm asking. I just have a strong feeling that I'm adopted."

My mother responded, "Don't be silly. You're not adopted. What, you want proof?"

I responded, "Well. Yeah." My mother opened the buffet drawer, pulled out paperwork, found my birth certificate, and showed it to me.

She pointed to the birth certificate, and said, "See? Our names are listed as your mother and father."

My father said, "Are you happy now?"

I answered, "Yeah." But I wasn't happy, and I wasn't fully convinced.

At that time, I didn't know about amended birth certificates, and that, after adoption, the original birth certificate is sealed, and a second, amended birth certificate is issued, citing the adoptive parents as the birth parents. Essentially, this created a false narrative of my life.

———

When my husband arrived, I showed him the baptismal certificate. He said, "Wow. Your mother is going to flip out." Then he added, "She was never gonna tell you this, but you had a right to know."

I nodded in agreement, and then I said, "You know what the weird thing is? I always felt that there was no way my mother – the person I thought was my mother – ever gave birth to me. There has always been a disconnect."

"Do you know what you're going to say to your mother?," he said.

I responded, "No. I have no idea. I just know that it's gonna to be impossible to stay calm."

After speaking with my husband, I phoned my mother, bypassed all pleasantries, and jumped right into the heart of the matter: "Hi mom. Do you know who Theresa P__ is?"

She paused and said, "No."

Well, apparently she's my biological mother, because her name is on my baptismal certificate."

There was a long pause. Then she said, "What are you talking about?"

"I just got my original baptismal certificate, and her name is listed as my biological mother." I paused, as I began to cry. I fought back to tears. "Am I adopted, mom?"

There was dead silence. Then she spoke, her voice quivering, "Oh my God. Who told you that? I'm calling the church! They had no right to tell you that!"

I raised my voice, saying, "Mom, answer me! I don't give a shit about the church. Is this true?!"

At this point, we were both crying, and her tears just verified that it really was true. I guess we were both angry and crying for different reasons.

"Yes, it's true," she said at last. "Let me explain... God damn it! They had no right to tell you this! You have to let me explain. Umm. I can't right now. I need to go. I don't feel well. I'm gonna call your aunt... I have to call your sister. I'll call you back in a little while." She hung up the phone, without offering me an explanation. By now, I was trembling.

Some time passed, during which I began to tell my husband what she said. Apparently, she phoned my aunt, because a few minutes later, the phone rang, and my Aunt Rita immediately reprimanded me, "Your mother just called me. She's very upset. You're gonna give her a heart attack. She's not a well woman!" My aunt didn't have an ounce of empathy for my feelings and my position.

Before I had a chance to respond to her, I heard the beep on my phone, indicating that another call was waiting. Since I didn't want to argue with my aunt, I said I had another call and I had to go.

The call was from my mother. "I just called your sister to tell her. Now she's upset too." She repeated, "They shouldn't have told you."

We were both still upset, and I wanted an explanation. I said, "Forget about what *they* told me. Why the hell didn't *you* tell me?!"

She said, "Your father and I didn't want to tell you, because we didn't want you to be upset, and feel that somebody didn't want you. I couldn't get pregnant, and we wanted a baby. We told you that you looked like us because we wanted you to believe you were part of the family. I never wanted you to find out."

"So you were *never* going to tell me?," I said. "And my whole life, I told doctors a medical history that wasn't even mine."

At this point, my heart was pounding and I began to cry again, "Mom, I'm too upset right now. I can't talk... I'm shocked... I'm mad. I'll call you back later." I hung up the phone.

After speaking with her, I decided to look through my Baby Book, since this is where the lies began. I read the entry which said that I had dimples like my father. (Years later, I learned that my birth mother also had dimples), my mother's smile, and my grandparents' features. The baby book created a story that biologically connected me to my adoptive family. Perhaps this was wishful thinking from my mother's perspective. To me, it was betrayal and deception.

I guess that as the years went on, more lies were created to validate other lies, and this complicated the situation. I think that it reached a point where there was no turning back, and it became impossible to tell me the truth.

I started to think about our ongoing tumultuous relationship. I was also told that I was Italian, and identified as such. Now I discovered that my birth mother was Irish. This new information regarding my ethnicity left me feeling raw, and my head was spinning. I thought to myself: *Who the hell am I?*

A few days later, my sister called. She said, "Mom told me, and I was shocked." Then she said that she told her sons, who were ten and twelve years old. She said that they asked her if they should still refer to me as *Aunt Nella*. She reassured them that nothing had changed. However, I still couldn't understand why she was having this conversation with her young children, and why she wanted to share this information with me, when I was already upset.

A few weeks passed after my first conversation with my mother. I was so angry, that nothing she could say would have helped me to feel better. Still, eventually I listened to her explanation. She said she and my father decided to keep this a secret, because they were afraid I would be upset, and I wouldn't be able to handle it.

She repeated that they really *wanted* a child, she had difficulty conceiving, and she felt blessed that she was given the opportunity to adopt me. It's ironic, because I never felt *wanted*. If I hadn't been abused and if had felt loved, I might have believed this explanation.

It took quite a while before I was able to come to terms with the fact that I was adopted, and I've never fully done so. Sometimes it still bothers me. It was difficult to get past this life-altering deception. Eventually I was able to reach some level of forgiveness for all involved, but it took a long time.

I decided that I wasn't going to search for my biological

mother or other biological relatives while my adoptive mother was still alive. Four years later, when she passed away, I began my search.

After hiring a private investigator to find my biological family, I learned that my biological mother was deceased. Apparently, she lived with my biological brother, about four blocks away from where I lived at the time. How bizarre is that? I felt sad to think that she lived so close to me, and we never had the opportunity to meet one another.

However, I was able to meet my biological siblings, my aunt, and my grandmother, and they were all kind to me. I still stay in touch with one of my brothers. He's a kind man, and has shared some of his beautiful memories of his mom – the woman who gave birth to me.

Here's my birth mother's story:

It was the 1950's. My biological mother was 17 years-old, and married for a year. Her husband was in the Korean war, and she became pregnant by another man. She lived with her husband's family, and this had to be stressful.

When her husband learned that she was pregnant, he told her that if she didn't put me up for adoption, he would leave her. He was not going to raise another man's child with her. My brother told me that she never forgave him for putting her in this position.

I can't imagine the anguish she must have experienced, living in a time where stigmas were attached to women in her circumstances. I wonder how many people in her family knew the real story concerning her pregnancy. I think about the heartbreak she must've felt when she signed the relinquishment paperwork.

———

Since I grew up in an Italian family, this heritage has been a huge part of my identity. This was my *tribe*. Therefore, when I first learned that I was adopted, and discovered that my birth mother was Irish, so I had Irish DNA, I struggled with this for a long time.

Eventually, I've come to define myself as Irish by birth, and Italian by circumstances. However, I identify as a woman of Italian descent, since I was raised in this culture.

Although this discovery put an additional rift in our already fractured relationship, eventually, I forgave mother, and we reconciled. Apparently she still held a grudge toward me, and I had no clue that, in that same year, she wrote her will, and decided to disinherit me.

My mother told other family members that she planned to take this secret "to the grave," and she was angry that I had discovered the truth. She was upset by my reaction, and couldn't understand why I felt that I had a right to be angry, because I was lied to. Instead, she saw *herself* as the victim.

From her point of view, since she adopted me, I should've been grateful. From my point of view, besides abusing me, I was deceived and lied to. Because of this lie, every time I went to a doctor, I gave a false medical history. She didn't think that this was a huge issue. I did.

It's hard not to think about *what-ifs*. I believe that if I had permanently severed ties with her after learning that I was adopted, I would have avoided the anguish I experienced four years later, when I learned that she disinherited me.

In 2020, New York finally passed a law allowing adoptees to receive their unamended, birth certificates, and other related documents. After decades of speculation, and signing petitions, I finally requested and received my documents, and, like everything else in my life, they were filled with some surprises.

I have one major regret in life that will always bother me. I was unable to meet my birth mother. From what I heard about her, according to my brother, she was a warm, kind-hearted, nurturing woman – someone I probably would have gotten along with and liked, and someone I might have even grown to love. There will always be a gaping hole in my heart in the shape of the motherly love that I've never received. No matter how old I get, it seems that it will always be there.

I have a fantasy. Well, it's more of a hope, that one day, when I cross over into the realm of the afterlife, I'll finally get to meet my birth mother. We will immediately recognize one another. We'll smile and say *hi* to each other. Maybe we'll hug one another. Maybe we'll shake hands. It doesn't really matter. – And then we'll sit down together and have a cup of coffee. We'll chit chat. I have no idea what we will say one another, and I don't think that matters either.

The point is that we will finally get to meet one another face-to-face. We'll connect. And maybe, just maybe, when this happens, that gaping hole in my heart that yearns for motherly love will finally be filled...

Chapter 22
Sisters

ONE OF MY FAVORITE TV SHOWS is called *Sistas*. It's about women who aren't blood related, but are close to one another – like sisters. Although they have disagreements, different personalities, and somewhat different world views, they still love and accept each other, and would never consider abandoning one another.

And then... I think about the troubled relationship that I had with my own sister, Stella, who is no longer in my life. Like the women in *Sistas*, we too, were dissimilar in so many ways. We've always had different interests, different friends, and different personalities. In fact, due to these differences, if we weren't sisters, we probably would have never chosen one another as a friend, since we had very little in common. .

Nonetheless, although our relationship was toxic, and she brought a lot of unnecessary drama and chaos into my life, as illogical as this sounds, there was a time when I loved her. However, it wasn't mutual. In hindsight, it saddens me to realize that although my sister always ended a conversation with the words "love you," her actions indicated that they were merely rhetorical, and never a true sentiment.

Besides, her version of love had too many conditions. These conditions caused me to slowly lose my self-respect and pieces of myself, as she continued to covertly abuse me. It took a long time to finally see that my relationship with my sister was stressful and poisonous, especially since, in many ways, she was exactly like my mother. Sadly, the toxicity had transcended generations.

In Louise DeSalvo's book, *Vertigo*, the author poses this powerful question: "How can a mother *mother*, when she hasn't herself been mothered?" Further, she asserts, "I never had a mother." Like DeSalvo, my sister and I were never *mothered* either.

Since my sister wasn't *mothered*, and was also abused, although she tried, she had no idea what it meant to be a loving mother, without conditions. Her children suffered because of this. It was inevitable that this cycle would continue to repeat itself. Like my sister, I wasn't *mothered* either. This is why I chose a different route, and made a conscious decision not to have children.

Who was the real Stella? I still wonder. We grew up together, even though, as children, we didn't socialize with each other, because we had vastly different interests. Still, we sat at the same dinner table, and lived in the same house for decades. Yet, I knew little about her as a person, and I guess the opposite is probably true.

I had no clue as to who Stella really was until my mother died, and she took all of my mother's possessions, refused to give me any of my mother's belongings, changed her phone number, and refused to speak to me. This behavior gave me insights into who my sister had become. Was she always this type of a person? Again, I don't know.

Then, after a ten-year estrangement, I made what I now consider to be a big mistake. Since I relocated to the same town where she lived, I decided to make an attempt at reconciliation, and hoped for the best. However, I didn't prepare for the worst.

During this period of reconciliation, I tried to ignore the toxic atmosphere in my sister's family, which replicated our family-of-origin: the gaslighting, the ongoing drama, the drug and alcohol abuse, the lack of healthy boundaries, the denial, the delusional thinking, the vindictiveness – it was all there. It was history repeating itself. It was frustrating to see that she was unable to connect the dots, and recognize that she too was a victim of abuse, and this replication was the fallout.

As I think back, I realize that I never really knew my sister, although I've had fantasies of who I wished she could be. I continued to hope that she would live up to these fantasies, even though a part of me knew that it was unlikely. There was so much evidence to the contrary.

If I had to describe my sister, based upon my experiences with her during our ten year reconciliation, this adage comes to mind: "Some people create their own storms, and then get upset when it rains." The problem was this: when I was within her sphere, this also brought me into her ongoing storms, and I got rained upon too.

In some ways, she was a chameleon, changing according to the situation. And she lied, one after another, even when there wasn't a reason to lie. This began in our childhood. Our parents encouraged us to tell the truth, but when we did, we were punished. Lying was how we protected ourselves from our parent's wrath. For Stella, this mechanism became a way of life.

———————

It was the Christmas season, and I was shopping for gifts...

"What size does Molly wear in sports shirts?" I asked Stella.

"Why?," she responded.

I explained, "Molly posted on Facebook that she enjoyed wearing sports shirts, so I thought this would be a perfect Christmas gift."

She answered, "No. Don't buy her that."

"I don't understand. Why?," I asked. There was silence, and she didn't respond.

I repeated, "Please just tell me what size she wears."

She responded, "Just give her money. She doesn't need any more sport shirts."

And this is typically how every holiday season went. My sister would dictate what I should and shouldn't give her adult children, and she complained if *she* didn't like the gift, or if she thought that I didn't give them enough money. They never complained.

She was the one who had the problem. For some reason, she was obsessed with the gifts that I gave to her adult children.

One Christmas, she called to complain on behalf of her son. "Hi, I just called to see how you're doin'. By the way, Jim really doesn't like the shirt you gave him. Can you return it and get the money, so you can give him the cash instead?"

Honestly, I was irritated, because some version of this happened every year. I took a breath, and then responded, "I don't have the receipt. I don't save receipts."

And she said, "Oh, that's OK, I'm just gonna throw it out then. I hope you don't mind."

I found her words offensive and provocative, but I wasn't going to give her the argument that she might have wanted. "Fine," I said. "I'm on my way out the door now, I'll talk to you later."

Her behavior reminded me of all the holidays with my mother, because the same sort of thing happened. She never liked the gifts she was given, and she always complained, because her birthday was two days before Christmas, and she said she "got cheated every year."

Sometimes I ask myself why I overlooked Stella's comments, and enabled her, rather than confronting her, and setting some strong boundaries. I think that I was empathetic because she too was damaged by our toxic family, and, honestly, I didn't like confrontation.

My mother-in-law would say, "We have to overlook things when we're in a family." As I've gotten older, I began to understand that some squabbles aren't worth a battle. But if the drama begins to pile up, we need to decide when to take a stand, and say, "Hey, this is enough!" I didn't do this. And, in not doing so, I became an enabler.

———————

It was June 22, 2019, and I just began dialysis. I was stressed and frightened, and could've used some support. I was invited to my nephew's house for a housewarming party.

Stella and I were sitting in the sunroom alone, and she began the conversation: "So, you started dialysis?" I nodded yes.

She continued, "Well, you know, just because you're on dialysis doesn't make my medical problems less serious. Even though, maybe, what I have is nothing compared to what you have, I still have big medical problems too."

I thought to myself, *What the hell?* I responded, "I don't know what you want me to say, Stella. It's not a competition."

"No. Of course not," she said. "I just wanted you to know that I'm going through a lot of crap too."

After this conversation, I had the feeling that she really *did* see this as a competition. At gatherings, Stella always considered herself the sickest one in the room, and she seemed to like it that way. The conversations were always about her new, self-diagnosed, perceived illnesses. If the conversation didn't focus on her maladies, she had nothing to say. Now, my illness was far more serious than any of the ones that she concocted, and this seemed to disturb her.

In a way, it's sad that she needed to create illnesses to get sympathy and attention. Yet, even this didn't seem to satisfy her.

Like my parents, she seemed to find comfort in being miserable. She constantly complained about how unhappy she was.

She was unhappy with her finances, even though she was well off. She was unhappy with her husband, because he was monitoring her expenditures, and he smoked marijuana daily. When her children and other relatives didn't behave as she wanted, she was unhappy with them too.

Aside from myself, her husband Robby was also a scapegoat, and she blamed him for almost everything that she hated about her life. But she never blamed my parents and our dysfunctional childhood. She couldn't make the connection between the negative childhood experiences that she endured, and the woman that she had become.

She's out of my life now, and, due to the final firestorm that she created, I see no path to reconciliation. And yet, there are still times when I miss her – or more accurately, I just miss the fantasy of who I wanted her to be. At the same time, I'm relieved, because it was overwhelming and stressful to be in a relationship with her. She was a human tornado, creating chaos wherever she went. I have no regrets, just disappointment. I'm trying to move away from disappointment and toward letting go and acceptance.

I feel I was the best sister I could possibly have been, especially during the worst period of her life, when I would often drop everything I was doing, because her daughter pleaded with me to spend time with her mother, who needed support. I did most of the giving, while she and her family did most of the taking. Regardless of how much I did, it was unappreciated and just never enough, which left me feeling exploited and used.

Although we live near one another, I only saw her on holidays, or when there was an occasion which required a gift. Other than that, I was never invited to her home, and she usually declined invitations to my home. However, she phoned me often, endlessly complaining. When one issue subsided, another dramatic event surfaced. She'd often say, "It's stressful to be in this family," unable to see that she was the one creating the unnecessary drama.

As I look back, I can see that some of the mistakes I've made with my mother were replicated in my relationship with Stella. First and foremost, I didn't enforce my boundaries, and didn't respond to the bullying. There were times when I kept silent rather than standing up for myself, which created an accumulation of resentments. That's on me.

I didn't recognize that I invested much time and energy in therapy to work through my childhood issues, but she didn't. She was stuck in the same unhealthy patterns, so essentially, we lived in two different realities. I also failed to see that since I was the scapegoat in my family, my sister continued to see me in this role, and continued to relate to me within the context of these unhealthy behavioral patterns.

Although I can empathize with her because she too was a victim of abuse, I also know that, like myself, she had an opportunity to get the necessary therapy to heal and move beyond this. She chose not to do so. Instead, she has chosen to cling to a perspective where she is always the victim, and is never responsible.

Further, she continued to scapegoat me, and ultimately, sent some of her family members to argue with me and threaten me. These unnecessary attacks contribute to why it's been so difficult to forgive her.

In hindsight, I realize my sister's version of love had too many conditions. These conditions caused me to slowly lose my self-respect and pieces of myself. It took a long time to finally see that my relationship with her was too stressful and toxic, especially since, in many ways, she was exactly like my mother.

It was only after my sister created an incredible firestorm, that I was able to see that it would be unhealthy to consider ever having a relationship with her again, because her toxicity was *infecting* my life. And now, I'm able to see that, although difficult and painful, this was the healthiest decision I ever made.

Looking back, I've learned that it's possible to care about someone, yet know that it's unhealthy to continue a relationship, unless they're willing to address the issues which have damaged it. The difficult part is letting go of the disappointment and anger. Nonetheless, I recognize that my heart needs to heal from this relationship, and I will continue to work toward forgiveness for my own well-being.

I have one final thought before closing this chapter. Despite the fact that I currently see no viable path toward reconciliation, there is still a part of me that will always care about my sister, even though I hate the way that she behaved toward me, and the pain that she inflicted upon me. Go figure...

Chapter 23
Dry Wells & Critical Voices

W HEN KENNY TOLD MY MOTHER he wanted to marry me, her response was, "Good. Now she can be *your* problem." In the history of asking parents for their blessings to marry their daughters, I can't imagine anyone ever responding like this. Yet, as far back as I can remember, I was labeled the "problem child," and she would often say, "I hope you have a daughter who is a pain in the ass, just like you were." I have no doubt that, regardless of my age, she would always see me that way.

I'm still amazed at how much credence I gave to her opinion of me. When I reflect upon our relationship, sometimes I envision a needy little girl shouting down a dry well, "Give me water! P-l-e-a-s-e," frustrated, and refusing to acknowledge that the well couldn't give what it did not have.

My mother was the dry well, and I adamantly refused to see that this dry well couldn't give me the nurturing and love that I so desperately needed and wanted. It wasn't going to happen, no matter how loud I yelled. But I just kept on yelling.

I guess you could say that I had a mixture of feelings toward her. I didn't hate her, but I hated the way that she behaved, and this disappointment morphed into anger. Like the child shouting in the well, I kept hoping she would surprise me and behave differently: maternal —supportive — loving. That didn't happen, and I was disappointed again and again. I'm reminded of Einstein's quote: "Insanity is doing the same thing, but expecting different results." That was me!

There were also other complexities inherent in this relationship. I cared about my mother with guarded reservation, because caring for her made me vulnerable. Experience had proven that each time I let my guard down, I gave her another opportunity to hurt me. And she repeatedly accepted this opportunity.

There were a few times when I tried to ignore her comments and innuendos, and took more of a passive, enabling stance. I thought this might stop her, but it didn't. Instead of backing off, my mother increased her hostile comments until she got the response that she was looking for – upsetting me or pissing me off.

Even after I was married, I remember feeling anxious whenever we spoke. The phone would ring, caller ID said it was her, and I'd feel the anxiety building up within me. Before answering the phone, I could feel my heart pounding, as I reached for my psychological armor and boxing gloves.

It's amazing that, after 24 years, I still remember her voice, especially the messages she left on my voicemail: "Hello Nell. It's mom. Is everything all right? I haven't heard from you. Did something happen to you?" I would think to myself, *something is guaranteed to happen*. I would return her call, with anxiety and great hesitation, and give her yet another opportunity to upset me.

She was so talented at being abrasive and disruptive. At times, when I confronted her about her criticisms, she would say, "Oh, come on, you can't take a joke. I was just kidding." Or, "I'm just trying to help you. You're too sensitive."

My mother was toxic, but, at the same time, she was also brilliant. No one could beat her at her own game. Her voicemail messages always sounded sincere. The subtle, sarcastic messages were brilliantly hidden within the recordings. Even her tone spoke volumes.

And so, year after year, we did the dysfunctional circular

dance, again and again: bickering, escalation, an explosion, estrangement, reconciliation. However, nothing was ever resolved. After a while, I internalized her ongoing criticisms, and eventually I struggled to see anything positive about myself.

And yet, my husband Kenny was always on my side, always supportive of me and complementing me. Still, I seem to be overpowered by my mother's criticisms, and gave less credence to Kenny's compliments. Her unrelenting verbal abuse overwhelmed me, and prevented me from feeling the love that was there for me elsewhere.

I consistently, often obsessively, stood by the dry well (that was my mother) pleading for water, while my husband had a well filled with an abundance of love. Maybe I was afraid. Maybe I found it hard to believe that I was lovable. Maybe it was difficult to receive love, because I didn't love myself. I've always found self-love a challenge.

I've often wondered what it would feel like if I could love myself like my animals have loved me – unconditionally, and with joyful gusto. I think about this when I'm playing with my dog, Alex, and the way he behaves towards me. Who wouldn't want to be adored? It's heartwarming – even heart-healing. When my dog gives me pure, unconditional love, and sees nothing negative in me, for those moments, I forget about all my perceived flaws, and I can see what he sees in me. It's an awesome feeling.

It's important to strive toward self-love. I'm reminded of a slogan in 12-step recovery groups: "Wherever you go, there you are." We can change the scenery around us, but we still have to live with ourselves. If we hate being in our own company, we can't run away from ourselves by getting on a plane and traveling elsewhere – because... well... there we are! Simple, funny, yet profound.

There was a time when I detested being in my own company. I tried to escape by using alcohol, but this was temporary, and only created bigger problems. It took a long time before I was able to like myself, and much longer before I could feel any love toward myself. It wasn't easy to get from point A to point B, especially when there were still echoes of that critical voice.

Much of my berating internal dialogue can be traced back to comments from my mother during my childhood years, and then, throughout my life. I still wonder, "Why did I give her the power to dictate what I believed about myself?" And then, being molested by my father further damaged my self-image and self-esteem.

My mother's negative observations, or what she called, *"I'm just trying to help you,"* affected me deeply, and greatly influenced how I saw myself. Was she deliberately trying to hurt me? It certainly felt calculated and intentional.

Her comments indicated that she disliked everything about me. Often, it felt like she hated me. My mother referred to me as *"Nell,"* and here were some of her common criticisms disguised as helpful hints:

- *Nell, you should fix yourself up.*
- *Nell, you need to put on some more make-up.*
- *Nell, I think you should comb your hair differently, because you have a high forehead.*
- *Nell, you should lose some weight.*

I don't understand how my mother criticized my weight, when she was obese. And yet, at the time, I never made this connection.

When I think back, I can't remember a single positive conversation with her which led me to feel good about myself. Rather, her critical words danced around my head over and over again. I gave her so much — way too much power over my feelings. I allowed her to make me feel diminished. To this day, sometimes I'm still bothered that our relationship was primarily defined by struggle.

Besides the stresses mentioned, I struggle with critical thoughts, nightmares and insomnia. Sometimes the more I try to fall asleep, the more wide awake I become. I envy my dog, Alex. He doesn't have insomnia. He closes his eyes, and within seconds, he's sound asleep. He lives in the moment. I don't know what his thoughts or dreams are about, but I'm pretty sure that he doesn't worry. He doesn't have resentments. He just forgives and moves on. I'm not as lucky as Alex.

Racing thoughts aren't confined to bedtime hours. Sometimes, I'll be having a pleasant day, then suddenly, without warning, my mood takes a nose dive. In AA, this is called wandering into "a bad neighborhood." Every day, I work hard to be mindful, and pay attention to the current moment. If I don't, my thoughts can easily swim around in the cesspool of yesterday's mistakes and tomorrow's possible catastrophes.

Recently, my inner voice has become far more loving, and less critical. I give myself credit where credit is due. If I make a mistake, I try to correct it, and learn from it, rather than beating myself up. Little by little, I'm becoming kinder to myself.

Over the years, I've learned that the most important relationship that I will ever have is with *me*. Other people will come and go. However, I have to live with myself every single moment of every day. When I was unhappy with myself, I lived an unhappy life.

Part of the self-love journey was learning how to give myself a break. I also had to forgive myself for poor choices and mistakes. Much of this work involved re-evaluating and discarding what I was told about myself when I was younger—reversing the brainwashing.

Chapter 24
The Rooms, & the 12 Steps

WHEN I WAS IN MY 30'S, I became overwhelmed by PTSD, flashbacks, and body memories regarding physical and sexual abuse. They would often happen simultaneously, and without warning. Body memories are uncomfortable body sensations that are related to the original trauma that was experienced. If a situation triggers a memory of a traumatic event, this can trigger uncomfortable bodily sensations that were experienced during the original trauma.

As mentioned before, there was a particular song that triggered a panic attack. Later, I remembered that this song was sometimes played when I was being molested. If I was in a supermarket when this song played, I would leave all of my groceries in the cart, and immediately exit the store. I knew that I had to put distance between myself and this triggering song.

It was a difficult and painful time in my life, and I would find myself reaching for a few glasses of wine to soothe my pain, and numb my feelings. Gradually, this unhealthy coping mechanism began to escalate. There were times when I would purchase a bottle of wine, open it, and then empty it into the sink, because I felt that I was losing control of my ability to stop drinking. I didn't want to admit this, but I was afraid of addiction.

I began to feel overwhelmed by the fear that my drinking was moving in a dangerous direction. And yet, it was still difficult to face the fact that I was developing a habit of abusing alcohol, because my drinking was confined to evenings and weekends, and didn't interfere with my work.

The counselor I was seeing at the time, suggested that I check out two different 12-step recovery groups: Alcoholics Anonymous (AA), for those who were struggling with alcohol abuse, and Adult Children of Alcoholics (ACoA), which helped people who grew up in alcoholic or substance-abusing families.

My counselor helped me to recognize that my parents had substance abuse issues. My father abused alcohol, and had a gambling problem, and my mother was addicted to tranquilizers and diet pills (amphetamines). We also talked about a *laundry list* – a list of personality traits common to children of alcoholic parents, and she helped me to see how I was affected by the addictive behavior of my parents. Since I'd been in therapy for a while, I already knew well many of the issues connected with my childhood experiences.

I didn't mind checking out an ACoA meeting. But AA? Eek! Not so much. It wasn't easy to look at my own struggles with alcohol. I never wanted to be anything like my parents. And yet, there I was, finding ways to escape life, just as they did. I felt humiliated, angry, and so disappointed with myself.

I struggled so much with the word *alcoholic*. Even though I didn't want to see myself as an alcoholic, I couldn't deny the fact that I was depending upon alcohol to numb my pain. Eventually, I went to a few ACoA meetings. However, my first stop was AA, and it was there that I found my tribe, and my place of refuge. Everything that I've learned in AA has been life changing, and has helped me to manage, deal with, and overcome every single challenge in my life.

On July 8th, 1988, I walked into my first Alcoholics Anonymous meeting, the first of many 12-step recovery group meetings that

I would attend over the years, which ultimately changed my life in miraculous ways.

"Hi, I'm Dianne," said the first person I saw, "Are you a newcomer?" I nodded yes. And then Dianne reached out to shake my hand. She smiled warmly, and said, "Welcome."

Dianne was the first person who greeted me, and I'll always remember this first warm encounter — one of many... And eventually I became the person reaching out my hand in friendship, and welcoming the next newcomer.

In this first meeting, I was particularly struck by the warmth of the energy in the room. Over the years, I've realized that this same warmth flowed through every single room and every meeting that I have ever attended.

The first meeting was memorable. I looked around and I saw men and women of all ages. Some were well-dressed, while others were dressed casually, wearing jeans and tee-shirts. They definitely didn't emulate my preconceived notion of what an alcoholic was supposed to look like. They looked like... well... they looked a lot like me.

The scene was nothing like I envisioned. I imagined I would see a few people who were intoxicated, and others who looked homeless, unkempt, and wearing tattered clothes. Instead, I saw people who seemed happy, some smiling and chatting with one another. I looked around, and thought to myself, "These people are alcoholics?"

There were two posters in the front of the room. One poster listed the 12 steps, and the other one listed the 12 traditions.

I tried to compare my experiences with the first step, and asked myself: Had I become powerless over alcohol? I wasn't completely sure, but a part of me knew that it was becoming increasingly difficult for me to stop drinking, once I began.

This indicated that I was headed toward being more and more powerless.

Was my life unmanageable? Hmm. I was dealing with a lot of flashbacks, PTSD, and emotional pain, that could only be *managed* by drinking. I said to myself, *C'mon, that's not really manageable.* In fact, the opposite is true. So, I had to admit to myself that, gradually, my life was becoming unmanageable.

I proceeded to read the second step. I had no problem believing that there was a power greater than myself. I've always called that power *God*. But... wait a minute – I read on: "restore us to sanity." I wondered, *What does that mean? Sanity?* I admitted that I was a little bit *out there*, even *quirky* at times, but the implication of *insanity* seemed extreme.

It took a while before I was able to understand the full meaning of this step. I was told that "insanity" was doing the same thing, but expecting different results. I thought that was an interesting definition. Did I ever do the same thing over and over, but expect a different result? Hell yeah!, I thought, *Okay, that fits.*

The third step referred to the Higher Power, as "God as we understood him."

Interesting. I have always believed in God, but I'd struggled, and still do, to identify with any particular religion. (See Chapter: Angels, Spirituality & Religion.)

This step, and their definition of God was extremely appealing to me. I loved a depiction of God which wasn't confined to rigid religious definitions. I thought to myself, *"Perfect! I can definitely live with that."*

My recovery journey began on that warm summer day in July. Over the years, I've learned that recovery isn't just about physical sobriety. The 12-step path also encompasses physical, psychological, and spiritual sobriety, or soundness of mind, body, and spirit. It's not simply about abstinence. That's just the beginning. The 12-step program is actually a way of life, a lifestyle change.

When people in recovery refer to "the rooms," they're talking about the fellowship, or the actual meetings that they attend. At these meetings, people share their "experience, strength, and hope," and within this sharing, magic happens. Others begin to identify with the speaker. They feel understood. They learn, grow, and recover. I know that I did, and I'm definitely not alone.

Over the decades, I've heard many stories where people were able to bounce back from the worst of circumstances. I've learned the true meaning of the words *resilience* and *inner strength*. I've seen what faith and hope can do. I've seen people walk into the rooms, beaten down by life , and in the depths of despair. Then, they slowly evolve into role models for others.

The fellowship is the place where people talk about how they apply the program in their lives, including the steps and the slogans. These all blend together to bring about recovery.

The first step asserts that we need to face the fact that we have an issue that is negatively impacting upon our lives, and we are unable to solve it alone. The second step proposes that we look beyond ourselves for help. The third step offers a spiritual solution. As I employed the first three steps into my life, I gradually began to feel much better.

The fourth and fifth steps are about taking personal responsibility for our lives, ceasing to blame others, and humbling ourselves. There are different interpretations of the fourth step, and what should be included in a searching and fearless moral inventory. My sponsor told me to write a list of flaws, mistakes I've made, things I might feel guilty about, as well as my assets and positive qualities. After making this inventory, in the fifth step, I shared this inventory with my sponsor, myself, and God.

The sixth and seventh steps are about being ready and willing to change, with God's help. It's about a shift in perspective, and complete trust in our Higher Power. It also includes a willingness to let go of control. Sometimes we become so comfortable with our flaws, that we're afraid to let go of them. The sixth and seventh steps help us to let go, and trust that God is going to help us.

The eighth and ninth steps address how our behavior has harmed other people. In the eighth step, we make a list of all the people that we've hurt, and acts for which we need to atone. To do so, we need to own our mistakes, and stop blaming others. In the ninth step, we do the work of atonement... making amends. This step was very difficult, but at the same time, it was very freeing.

The tenth, eleventh and twelfth steps are about ongoing accountability, where we continue to atone for mistakes that we might make, continue to seek help and guidance from our Higher Power, try to live a spiritual and moral life, and help others.

After the ninth step, the *Big Book* of AA talks about "the promises" that many people in the program experience, after they complete this step. I was able to identify with many of them. I've experienced a sense of freedom. I saw of value of past experiences. I began to capture glimpses of serenity, clarity of thought returned, and I saw the value of helping others, simply by sharing my own experience, strength, and hope.

The most important promise, and one which has followed me throughout my life, talks about realizing that God is doing for us what we cannot do for ourselves. God has, and continues to be the guiding force in my life.

There have been so many times when I felt like I didn't have an ounce of strength to address a challenge I was facing. And then, suddenly, I've been able to overcome some very difficult circumstances. This experience is God taking charge of my life, and guiding me in the right direction. Each time, I have been able to feel the power of God.

There are also many slogans, but the slogan *one day at a time* has helped me the most, when I was confronted with obstacles. Over the last few decades, the only thing that helped me to survive one chunk of adversity after another, was knowing that I could do anything for 24 hours. I continue to follow this credo to this day, and take life *one day at a time*. Sometimes it's *one minute at a time*, but that's okay too.

The most important thing that I've learned was that I could deal with adversity, even the worst of circumstances, without reaching for a glass of wine, or other forms of escapism. However, I've learned so much more: how to live life on life's terms, acceptance, the power of prayer, and many other coping tools.

Over the last 34 years, I've successfully used everything that I've learned in AA, and then, ACoA (Adult Children of Alcoholics), including the steps and slogans, to address and overcome every single challenge in my life.

There's another slogan that I often draw upon to help me through the tough times: *Don't give up a minute before the miracle happens*. These words of encouragement have dwelled in my heart ever since I first heard them decades ago. I have carried this slogan with me through many challenges, and they have helped me through countless difficult and dark moments.

Even when I might initially feel devastated by unexpected obstacles, the idea of giving up has never been a serious option for me. This doesn't mean that I didn't experience moments when I was extremely depressed. Nonetheless, eventually I was able to bounce back from that dark place.

What exactly is "the miracle"? Volumes of books have been written about the nature and various aspects of miracles. One explanation that I particularly like comes from *A Course in Miracles*, written by Helen Schucman, which defines a miracle as a change in perception. When our perception changes, our world and our circumstances look completely different... that's the miracle.

In my experience, this shift in perception has often melted away my fears, and allowed me to look at a situation from a broader perspective. Within this miracle, I have been given the capacity to open my eyes, and to see the hope of infinite possibilities that had previously eluded me

Imagine walking into a dimly lit room. There are many things that you can't see, but they are still there. Then, suddenly, a bright light emerges to illuminate the darkness, and you are shocked to see everything that, just a second ago, was invisible. New insights fill the room! When your perception shifts, so do your choices and your future. And... that's huge.

A few years into recovery, I wrote this poem which explained my experiences with alcohol:

Master of Deception
It was liquid courage,
reckless bravery.
It was a pseudo-scholar –
a guru of con-artistry.

It was a fantasy lover,
Charming and romantic.
It was calmness – it was excitement.

Tranquilizing – frantic.

It was a pseudo-parent,
Nurturing the emptiness.
It was a living hell,
Creating pain and distress.

It was a spiritual undertaker,
Laying the dead soul to rest.
It distorted human potential,
Enhancing worst – destroying best.

It was the worst depth of insanity.
A fluid snake pit – Exit-less.
It was suicide of the soul,
Making life feel meaningless.

It was a slow consuming cancer,
A ruthless killer, with lies to tell.
It was a demon dressed as a prophet,
Promising heaven, emitting hell.

It was dressed in fancy clothing,
Skull and crossbones concealing.
It was sensuous and alluring,
Seductive and appealing.

It would take you to the depths of ecstasy,
Then send you crashing down unmercifully –
Causing you to die in fragments...

It was a master of deception...
It was alcohol...

Chapter 25
Angels, Spirituality & Religion

IT WAS THE SUMMER OF 2019, and I was bummed out because I had just started dialysis. As I glanced through the list of TV shows, one title caught my attention. The show was called, *Touched by an Angel*. I thought about the 12th promise in AA literature, "We will suddenly realize that God is doing for us what we could not for ourselves." Since I believe that God guides us, and sends us messages to help us, I wanted to check out this show.

Since I believe in angels, and God's unconditional love, I watched one episode, and I was captivated. I've been watching this show for a while now, including repeats, and it continues to inspire me. It has helped me to cope with the last few years of my life, as I adjusted to being on dialysis, and the difficult lifestyle and dietary changes that came along with it.

The show focuses on angels in human form, who are sent by God to help people who are struggling in certain areas of their lives. Often the stories are sad. However, all that I see when I look at this show is Inspiration and Hope.

The first message to each struggling person in the show is, "God loves you." Simple yet powerful. There have been times when it's been difficult to believe that God loves me. In those moments, I wondered if I was being punished for something. I believe this is due to 12 years of a parochial school education and indoctrination. The good news is that I've moved beyond this restricted thinking.

I never really accepted a depiction of God as hateful or

vindictive – a punishing God. The God of my understanding is a loving God, similar to the New Testament God that Jesus spoke about. The message from these angels in *Touched by an Angel* wasn't difficult for me to believe. In fact, it was very comforting. Throughout my life, I believe that God has always loved me, strengthened me, and helped me.

Although I've watched every episode repeatedly, every time I hear the words, "God loves you," it still warms my heart. I can deeply feel the love in these words. I need this reminder. It helps me get through every moment of every day, especially dialysis days, or days when I feel I don't have even a smidgeon of energy or hope, or days when I wonder if I will ever get a kidney transplant, and return to some normalcy.

I'm also touched by the powerful words in the theme song, *I Will Walk with You*, beautifully interpreted by Della Reese. The lyrics assert that God will walk with us, regardless of what's going on in our lives. I believe that we're never really alone, even if we might feel that way. This song reminds me of the poem *Footprints in the Sand* (author unknown), which says that God has always walked with us and carried us, especially through the most horrible moments of our lives.

In 12-step groups, we're told not to compare our stories, but rather, to identify with the sentiments in the stories being shared. This is how I approach this TV show. I can always identify with the feelings depicted in each story. I know what it's like to be immobilized by fear, or to feel alone, even in the presence of other people, including loved ones. I know what it feels like to think about the future, and see only darkness. On the other hand, I believe that God loves me, is with me, and gives me courage, resilience, hope and strength. God didn't take me this far to desert me.

One final thought before closing this section. In one of the episodes, Wynona Judd sings a beautiful song called: *Testify to Love*. She talks about the beauty of God's creation, citing, among other observations, the beauty of colorful rainbows, and the elegant, twinkling stars in the sky. She closes the song with these heartfelt words: "With every breath I take, I will give thanks to God above."

In my experience, the knowledge that God loves me, and walks with me, continues to assist me in rising above the circumstances that I find myself in, and so, despite the challenges in my life, like Winona, I, too, am grateful.

———————

Before I expanded my views on spirituality, I was raised in the Catholic religion, and went to a Catholic grammar school and high school...

"Go across the street and give the envelopes to your Aunt Teri, so she can throw them in for us." My aunt and her family went to church every Sunday, while my parents didn't go to mass very often, except for Good Friday, Christmas, and Easter. Instead, my mother put money in the weekly envelopes so my aunt would put them in the offering basket —*throw them in* – for our family. Often, my sister and I attended mass with our classmates during the week.

If my parents didn't give weekly donations, then we would no longer remain in good standing with the church. My mother didn't want this to happen, because my sister and I attended Catholic school. She would comment, "They want their money," or, in a joking way, "We don't wanna get kicked out." As funny as this sounds, it was the truth. If parishioners didn't give weekly donations to the church, then their children would not be allowed to remain in Catholic school.

Sometimes my parents would try to justify why we didn't to go to mass, by citing their grievances. In an annoyed tone, my father would toss his hands in the air, and say, "It's the handshaking. I'm not gonna shake hands with someone I don't know."

My mother had a different reason: "Your father works hard all week. He's tired. Can't expect him to get up early on Sunday just to go to church."

"That's right," he would agree.

Both of my parents had an ongoing feud with the church, when they decided to remove the statues of the saints: My mother would say, "What's wrong with them? They kicked out all the saints."

"What the hell? It's a shame," my father would chime in. This was probably one of the few things that they agreed on.

I didn't care what their reasons was were, I was just happy that I didn't have to go to church every Sunday. In the 1960s, churches didn't have air conditioners in the summer. Instead, there were two huge fans that re-circulated hot air all round the room. The church was as hot as an oven.

Some parishioners perspired profusely, as they wiped their faces with their handkerchiefs, while others used the church bulletins to fan themselves. Some rolled their eyes, while others sighed.

———

Although I went to Catholic school for 12 years, I've always had the inclination to be a spiritual boundary crosser, and throughout my life, I've explored different religions, much to the dismay of my mother. "I paid all that money to send you to Catholic school, and you're studying other religions?," she would lament. Even though she didn't go to mass a lot, Catholicism was important to her.

I felt differently. Unlike her, I didn't believe that if you were born one religion, you had to remain that religion for the rest of your life. I respect all spiritual paths to God. Throughout my life, I've studied the sacred texts of various religious traditions. In each of them, there were beautiful, inspirational words of wisdom and comfort.

I identify myself as spiritual rather than religious. I believe in a Higher Power, who has always walked with me and strengthened me through every single struggle in my life.

The God of my understanding is a God of Love, not a punishing God. My connection with God extends beyond the limitations and the parameters of any religion. I think that God is way too big to be confined to any one theological doctrine. But I still see myself as a woman of faith.

Although I don't watch the televangelists, which are religion-based, I do watch Super Soul Sunday, hosted by Oprah Winfrey. This show approaches God and faith from a broad, multi-faith, spiritual perspective.

"What is the soul?" This is the question Oprah asked different guests on her show, and each person shared a heartfelt answer. I've reflected upon my own definition, so here's my two-cents-worth.

I feel that the *soul* is God's signature, which exists within the heart of every living being, including animals. It isn't material or physical. It can't be measured or identified through human means, because it comes from the spiritual realm. And yet, it's equally discernible. I can feel God's presence within me with the same intensity that I can feel my own heartbeat.

I experience God in different ways. Sometimes I sense God's

presence in the form of gentle guidance, comfort, and hope. I also feel the presence of God in the physical world – in the beauty of nature. I feel God in every rainbow, every blooming tree in the spring, every flower that grows, every gentle summer breeze, and every beautiful, graceful butterfly that crosses my path. In the evening, I've seen God's signature in the beautiful colors of a magnificent sunset. Every animal companion in my life has also given me a glimpse of God through their unconditional love.

Writer Patrick Overton beautifully describes faith with these words: *"When you have come to the edge of all light that you know, and are about to drop off into the darkness of the unknown, faith is knowing one of two things will happen: there will be something solid to stand on, or you will be taught to fly."*

I share his sentiments. There were times in my life when I was bombarded with obstacles, and experienced the *"the darkness of the unknown."* As I stood in this place, somehow, I just knew... *I just felt...* that I was *not* going to topple off a cliff, and if I did, then a power greater than myself would catch me before I hit the ground. Since I'm still standing, apparently *someone* did. Thus far, regardless of what has happened in my life, God has always given me the strength to handle it.

Why are we here? This is a question I've often asked myself. Since no one really knows, any answer would be speculation or just one's personal perspective.

For argument's sake, if we were a pure *spirit* or a *soul* that existed before we took human form, the more interesting existential question might be: *Where were we before we became confined to a body?* Now, that's fascinating! I'm going to share my theory.

Perhaps we temporarily gave up dwelling in the realm of paradise, and chose human form, so that our souls could evolve by experiencing different life challenges in the physical world.

Regardless of the reason, I'm here now, I need God's help, and I get this help through my spiritual connection with my Higher Power through various prayers.

Dear God, please help me to evolve and become better versions of myself, according to your will. I say this prayer every day. Since I'm different than I was a few years ago, I'm guessing that this prayer is being heard and answered. I also understand that I need to do the footwork.

When I open my eyes in the morning, I have chronic pain. I need to get up and walk around a little, so it can subside. My attitude isn't always pleasant when I first open my eyes. I try to counteract this by saying what I call *the attitude adjustment prayer:*

Dear God, thanks for giving me this day. I understand that it's a gift from you to me. Help me to use it well, with a positive attitude, and possibly to bring a little bit of happiness into someone else's life.

There have been trying times in my life when my prayer was simply, *God, please help me,* accompanied by tears. I think that the sentiments are more important than the spoken words, because God already knows what our hearts feel. I'm reminded of a quote by writer Kathe Wunnenburg, *"There is a holiness about your tears. Each one is a prayer that only God can understand."*

I think that sometimes God answers prayers by calming the storm, but other times, he allows the storm to continue. In those cases, he answers our prayers by giving us the inner strength to withstand the storm, gain wisdom, and identify the learning lessons.

I was first introduced to The Serenity Prayer in 12-step recovery groups. It reads: *"God, grant me the serenity to accept the things I cannot change, the courage to change what I can, and the wisdom to the difference."*

Serenity... courage... and wisdom... Although none are easy, I've struggled the most with accepting that which I was powerless to change, and the ability to discern what I could and could not change.

There is also an extended version of this prayer, that I can relate to, and it coincides with the 12 steps of AA:

Living one day at a time;
Enjoying one moment at a time;
Accepting hardship as the pathway to peace;
Taking this world as it is, not as I would have it;
Trusting that God will make all things right
if I surrender to His Will;
That I may be reasonably happy in this life,
and supremely happy with Him in the next.

The first time I read the St. Francis prayer in AA literature, although the words were beautiful, I thought that it seemed impossible to achieve. At second glance, I could see that this prayer was about progress rather than perfection. Each verse is something to strive toward in order to grow as a spiritual person. When I say this prayer, I begin to feel a soothing effect.

God, make me an instrument of your peace
Where there is hatred, let me sow love.
Where there is injury, pardon.
Where there is doubt, faith.
Where there is despair, hope.
Where there is darkness, light.
And where there is sadness, joy
O Divine Master, grant that I may not so much
seek to be consoled as to console
To be understood, as to understand.
To be loved, as to love.
For it is in giving that we receive.

And it's in pardoning that we are pardoned.
And it's in dying that we are born to Eternal Life.
I discovered this next prayer accidentally, and found the imagery vivid and comforting.

Here are some excerpts from St. Patrick's Breastplate Prayer:
I arise today, through the strength of heaven,
The light of the sun,
The radiance of the moon,
The splendor of fire,
The speed of lightning,
The swift of wind,
The depth of the Sea,
The stability of the earth,
the firmness of rock.

I arise today, through God's strength to pilot me,
God's might to uphold me,
God's wisdom to guide me,
God's eye to look before me,
God's ear to hear me,
God's word to speak for me,
God's hand to guard me,
God's shield to protect me
God's host to save me
from snares of devils,
from temptation of vices,
from everyone who shall wish me ill,
afar and near.

One of the AA traditions talks about striving toward progress rather than perfection. This is how I view spirituality. I try to make progress each day to be a better person than I was the day before. It's a lifelong journey, and at times, difficult.

One day at a time, I continue to maintain my faith. It's not always easy, especially during weeks when I experience one obstacle after another, coming at me, without an end in sight. But since I've been on this Earth for more than a minute, I've learned that every situation, good or bad, is transient.

Sometimes my husband will comment on how incredible it is that, although I go through so many obstacles in my life, I still have faith, I find comfort in praying, and I still believe that God helps me. I found this poem called *The Master Weaver's Plan*, (author unknown), that explains my sentiments:

My life is but a weaving
Between my God and me.
I cannot choose the colors
He weaves so steadily.

Sometimes he will weave sorrow;
And I, in foolish pride
Forget He sees the upper
And I the underside.

Not until the loom is silent
And the shuttles cease to fly
Will God unroll the canvas
And reveal the reason why.

The dark threads are as needful
In the weaver's skillful hand
As the threads of gold and silver
In the pattern He has planned

He knows, He loves, He cares;

Nothing this truth can dim.
He gives the very best to those
Who leave the choice to Him.

In the prayer composed by St. Nicholas of Flüe, he talks about how our ego can distance us from God: "Lord and my God, take from me everything that distances me from You... give me everything that brings me closer to You... detach me from myself in order to give my all to You."

Regarding the ego, sometimes the smallest prayer is the most profound: "Dear God, more of you, less of me."

In the song, *Rocky Mountain High*, in a few powerful words, John Denver beautifully talks about his views on prayer: "Talk to God and listen to the casual reply." I love the idea that God responds to our prayers in a *casual*, almost relaxed and calm way. When I hear these words, I think about a loving parent, calming a child, and letting the child know that everything is going to be okay.

Chapter 26
Grieving Losses

'VE NEVER DIED FROM EMOTIONAL PAIN, or drowned in my tears, although, at the time, it felt as if I would. And yet, when I was consumed by grief, sometimes the feelings... darkness... emptiness... have been beyond description.

In my experience, grief is really about powerlessness. We have lost someone or something that is valuable to us – someone or something we love and need – perhaps it's someone or something that we feel we can't live without, and we can't do a damned thing about it. That emptiness becomes filled with palpable sorrow and heartbreak. The weird thing is that recent grief always seems to stir up memories of all my other losses, and I've had quite a few. While writing this, as I browsed through my life, I was able to see that there are some similarities in *all* losses.

On September 10th of 2020, my beloved Bassett hound, Penelope, crossed over into the afterlife, and I was deeply heart-broken. As I'm writing this chapter, it's September 9th, 2021, and I'm reminded that tomorrow will be one year since she left the physical world. Penelope was beautiful, with multi-colored fur – white, brown, and black, and expressive, soulful eyes.

Although I believe that her spirit, and everyone's spirit lives on, and we will reunite in the afterlife, I miss Penelope's physical presence, I'm saddened by this anniversary, and I'm reminded of the pain and heartbreak I felt because of this loss. Penelope was smart, yet stubborn. She had her own mind, and she didn't like to be told what to do. In that sense, she and I were alike. She had a big personality, and she helped me to change and grow as a person in significant ways. She will never be forgotten. Every day, I talk to her in her spiritual form, because I believe that she is still with me.

I have her urn with her ashes on my mantlepiece, but I still cannot associate her ashes with who she was. A year later, it's still extremely painful to look at, or touch, her collar. I have it in a plastic Ziplock bag. Sometimes I'll take a whiff, and I swear I can still smell her scent – that distinctive hound smell.

Most of the time, I'm able to look at her photographs and videos, and smile, recalling some happy memories of her antics. For example, often my husband Kenny put his coffee cup on the floor, and Penelope would mosey on over and casually take a little sip. She understood much of what we said, and if I was making a vet appointment for her, she would run into the other room. One time we rolled a bowling ball on the floor, and she ran after it, trying to catch it. It was hilarious. She was an interesting and silly girl.

Sometimes I'm happy that I have videos. I can watch them and smile. But then, there are other times I'm overwhelmed with sadness. There are times when I can't even glance at her photographs without bursting into tears. I guess that's grief. It's not a straight line moving forward. Rather, the emotions bounce back-and-forth.

Like other pet parents, I know that I will probably outlive my adopted animals. I know that my happiest *hello* will someday be my saddest and most painful *goodbye*. However there's a big difference between *knowing* something and *experiencing* it. Also, since her loss was sudden, it was even more upsetting. I still miss her. I talk to her spirit, saying good morning when I wake up, and good night at the end of the day. This brings me some comfort.

When I try to remember the joyful moments, the silly

things she did, and the ten years that we've spent together, my thoughts always default to the events surrounding the last day of her life. Why?

In allowing myself to be vulnerable by loving an animal, or a person, I know that one day, I might feel the pain of loss. The greater the love, the deeper the grief. Since animals love us unconditionally, we share a unique type of love with them.

Animals love us like no human being can. They love us regardless of our mood. We can't hide our emotions from an animal. They know if we're hurting, and they are 100% empathetic. They love us more than they love themselves.

If I could go back, I wouldn't change a thing, because I enjoyed and learned so much from the years I've shared with Penelope. She was stubborn and frustrating at times, as well as cute, lovable, silly, and goofy. My husband and I gave her a good and happy life, and took great care of her. She taught me so many life lessons, and helped me to grow in significant ways.

Regardless of the circumstances, all grief is gut-wrenching. The worst part is that it's not linear, with a beginning, middle, and end. It's more of a dance. I've taken a few steps forward, and then slipped backward, bouncing through different stages once again.

I might feel acceptance today, only to find myself angry and depressed again tomorrow. Grief has led me through a bumpy path, with winding roads and u-turns. I've been through much grief and different types of losses throughout my life. I've felt a deep sorrow, because I never had the opportunity to meet my birth mother. I've also grieved the losses incurred because my childhood years were filled with fear and abuse, which has left me with irreparable wounds. There are times when I still feel twinges of this grief – a gnawing sadness of could-have-beens, should-have-beens, and what-ifs.

My more recent experiences with grief involve my loss of health, and my need to be on dialysis. This has been huge! Unless you've come face-to-face with a serious and life-threatening illness, it's hard to explain the barrage of feelings, and the fear and stress of this life-altering journey. Over the past few years, I've bounced back and forth through the stages of grief, and I've learned the deepest meaning of the word *powerless*.

Since some time has passed, I have become more accepting of my health issues, or, more accurately, the lack of health. I still have moments when I feel depressed and frustrated, or I think, *why me?* I still cry at times, but I try to give myself a time limit. Sometimes I wonder if I'll live long enough to get a transplant. Then I try to tell my mind, *"Don't go there!"*

The good news is that I'm still here, and I have a responsibility to make the best of the time that I have. As much as I would like to stop dialysis, I can't, because I know that I'll die, and I'm not ready to do so just yet. I have much more that I want to accomplish, and more books to write. If I give up, then I'm letting the disease win this battle, and I refuse to let that happen! I've never backed away from a fight in my life, and I'm not going to do so now.

Even in the midst of heartbreaking grief, there are times when I'm still able to capture a glimpse of the preciousness of each moment. I've also become cognizant of how many moments I've wasted. I think about the stupid things I've worried about in the past. They seemed so monumental at the time, but now they seem so trivial. This raises the question: how important we're they in the first place?

———————————

The Buddhists talk about impermanence, and say that attachment always gets us into trouble. We go through life grabbing one thing after another, hoping that it will bring us some happiness. Then we suffer, because we can't accept that everything is impermanent. Everything is on loan to us. We own nothing, including our health.

I was deeply saddened to learn that I needed to be on dialysis, and I had to grieve many losses. The symptoms of this disease are overwhelming. I feel chronically fatigued, often nauseated, and after dialysis, shortness of breath. My emotions vacillate. I feel anxious, especially on scheduled dialysis days. I'm frightened that I'm never going to get a transplant. Acceptance comes and goes. I'm angry, sad, and frustrated, that I am in this position. I have to work hard to keep my thoughts in the current moment.

My grieving process went through a few stages. Although I knew my kidney disease was getting progressively worse for nearly a decade, when my doctor told me I needed dialysis, I was still stunned. As the shock subsided, I began to feel guilty, and I blamed myself because I felt that I might have contributed to my kidney disease. It still took a while before I could let go of self-blame and forgive myself.

As I moved past the sadness, I became angry, and felt betrayed by my own body. I became depressed because I couldn't change my situation. It helped me to reach out to God for comfort, strength, and resilience. Eventually, I became more comfortable with my *new normal*, and started having more good days than bad days. However, I still bounce back and forth. I also continue to work hard at staying in the present moment, and live one day at a time.

In 12-Step recovery literature, there is a beautiful excerpt concerning acceptance. Briefly, acceptance is seen as the answer

172 I Dancing in the Rain

to all of our frustrations. The passage asserts that we cannot find peace and serenity until we are able to accept situations that we are unable to change. That's so true!

I never thought that I could adjust to being on dialysis. I still have moments when I feel sad, frustrated, and just plain angry. Three days a week, I need to get out of bed, get dressed, and go to the dialysis center, and sometimes it feels like a part-time job. I never expected that, in my retirement years, this would be a part of my life.

Often, I need to remind myself that dialysis is prolonging my life, and everyone has challenges. The truth is, it can always be worse. One day at a time, I continue to enjoy my life within the parameter of these new normals.

Chapter 27
Dry Tears & Poetry

I DON'T REMEMBER SHEDDING many tears when I was growing up, yet, my heart was bleeding sorrow and hopelessness. I think that my sadness morphed into words on a page. My tears dripped onto the blank looseleaf sheet, became a poem, and then evaporated and disappeared. But the thing is, they really didn't disappear completely, they just hid inside a closet, and impacted upon my life in covert, yet powerful ways.

Writing poetry was the only way I was able to vent and give expression to my emotions – the only way I could document my journey – my feelings – my pain – my relevance – my reason for being. Every tear immersed in every word had an important tale to tell.

A few poems in this chapter were written when I was a child. Sadly, due to relocating, many of my earlier writings have been lost. Years later, when I was re-exploring some of my childhood pain in therapy, I wrote other poems. (Most of the poems in this chapter are excerpts of larger poems.)

The Colors of Sadness
The colors of sadness are putrid green and rusty brown.
Salty tears burn my heart.
The land of Oz is so far away,
The yellow brick road, obscured.
And magic potions aren't real.
Sad realities engulf and devour me.

I feel like the weather today...
– dim and cloudy.
Or... does the weather feel like me?

Lonely in a crowd,
Tasting solitude.
Desolate despair...
Teeming tears...
Endless fears...

The colors of sadness engulf and devour me.

Shades of Solitude
The deep colors of loneliness grasp me.

I am in a trance, suspended within time and space.
Aloneness...
nothingness...
darkness...
These are my shades of solitude.
They cannot hurt me...

The Dark Years... A Little Girl's Tears
There was a time, perhaps when I was age three or five,
When joy was a possibility in my life.
I dreamed of beautiful flowers in bright garlands,
until reality coldly severed it like a knife.

Then the leaves turned brown,
and they looked so sad,
And a gray dark cloud prevailed
where the sun once smiled.

Santa Claus and the Easter Bunny died.

So I was left all alone
to handle things on my own.

I once thought life could be like the land of Oz.
Perhaps when I was still yet in the crib.
And then life became a cold and hellish web,
With anguish, lies, and no way to get out.

But there was a time before this little girl's tears,
When I felt joy was a real possibility in my life.
And now the past does not have to exist,
If I could only extinguish it from my mind.
And perhaps this will be the only way to find
The joy I wanted, before all of those dark years.

Swept Away

I would cling to the passing wind,
Hoping to be swept away.
But no magic solutions did I find
that could soothe my dismay.
They were Swept...Swept, Swept...Away...

Immersed in the quicksand of aftermath,
The deep darkness obscured my path,
and the frightening thought
of Another Day.... And Another Day... And Another Day...

I had dreams of rescues and being saved,
But Don Quixote was busy fighting windmills,
and Batman hid in the bat cave,
frightened and no longer brave.
I felt saddened and stranded
by hope abandoned ...

Shouting whispered pleas
To those who looked the other way.
Appeals just echoed and blew away,
like beach sand on a windy day.
Going... Going... Gone...

Teary-eyed and waving goodbye,
As hopes melted in the sun...
One by One... One by One...
Until One became None...

Hope was swept to the curb,
and washed away by the rain,
Again...and again... and again...

Scraps of Sadness (excerpt)

My heart was once a grand ocean
of salty tears that continued to flow –
I still remember that little girl,
Who lived in what feels like a lifetime ago.

Sadness feels like a delicate flower,
Vulnerable and helpless,
Caught in the cusp of a tornado,
Struggling every waking hour.

Is the weather dark and dreary today?
Or... Is that just a reflection of the burden in my heart?
I was just a lost soul, trying to survive another day...

Windswept (excerpt)

So here I am again...
Powerless once more,
And frightened to the core.

The facts of life are bold,
Insensitive and cold.
They've clutched me by the throat,
Forcing me to kneel.
They don't care what I feel!

Do struggles ever end?
Alas, I'm windswept one again.
I feel windswept once again...

If wisdom's born of struggle,
Does it ever really show?
Do we see it as vibrant fireworks,
Or simply a soft glow?

As the darkness bows to light,
And the day banishes the night,
When... If... I finally understand,
will I feel the depth of insight?

Do insights transcend time and space?
Do the puzzle pieces fall in place?
If I reach a higher plane
with less losses and more gains,
When I finally find the answers,
Will I be the last to know?

Snapshots through Time (excerpt)
As the years spin in my mind,
Like snapshots on a carousel —
The whirling randomly stops,
Allowing me to see
What was — what is — the total me...

Bits and pieces meshed together
Through the years – rusted by tears.
Cloudy thoughts now seem a hazy dream.
Did yesterday really exist?

Happiness as fluid as the sand,
Quickly slipping through your grasping hand,
And it slides through your fingers so quickly,
that the experience is lost.

Lessons that I've learned so deeply
have rendered me consumed with pain completely.
At that moment, feeling I would die,
But somehow, I continued to survive.
But do I feel – more or less alive?

Walking away from Hell
It could have been so different,
The way you treated me.
You could have shown some kindness
And been a mom and dad to me.

As I remember could-have-been's
Almost obsessively
I can't stop my tears from gushing,
And the pain that flows through me.

So thanks a lot for
The enduring pain I'm left to bear.
And as I walk away from hell,
 I hope you both remain there...

Carousels
Grief and loss, regrets and tears,
Can weigh heavily upon the years.
The carousels that used to shimmer,
Now weary, tired, and so much dimmer...

Chapter 28
The Dialysis Journey

ELLA, YOU NEED TO BE ON DIALYSIS."
Dr. Capicotto's words began a new, life-changing journey for me. I will never forget them. And yet, I expected to hear this horrible news. Before my appointment, I looked up my bloodwork results online, and I already knew that my creatinine was skyrocketing, and my kidneys were functioning below 10%. Physically, I began to feel sick. I was nauseated. I was vomiting. I was itchy. Since I Google everything, I knew that these symptoms meant that my kidneys were quickly getting much worse.

"*God damn it!,*" I thought to myself, as I read my recent bloodwork.

Then I thought, *Maybe the bloodwork is wrong.* I kept looking at the page on my iPad, thinking that, if I stared long enough, it would suddenly change. At the same time, I knew that I was trying to bullshit myself.

Maybe I should cancel my appointment. I thought that avoiding this appointment would somehow prolong the inevitable.

I shared my blood work results of my husband, Kenny, and asked, "So, do you think I should cancel my appointment? "

"What? What good will that do?" He paused, then continued, "It's not gonna change anything, is it? Just go and get it over with. It sounds like you already know what he's gonna say."

I thought, *I know what my nephrologist is going to say. I just don't want to hear it.*

And so, reluctantly, I got into the car, and we both went to see my doctor.

My nephrologist is a tall, good looking man, with black longish hair, and a neatly trimmed mustache and beard. He is of Italian-American descent, so we have a lot in common. He is likable in so many ways – personable, charming, empathetic, witty, compassionate, highly intelligent, and totally authentic. He also emits a very calming presence. This man can walk into a dreary dialysis unit, and get each patient to crack a smile. He's just a lovable guy, and he treats each of his patients like family.

On this particular day, although his voice was compassionate, not even he could soothe the alarming, life-altering news he had to give me. Although I expected this outcome, each word still felt like sharp knives coming at me, plunging into me, one by one.

Then these words floated and lingered in the air, waiting for me to process them. I just didn't want to hear the word "dialysis" and my name, used in the same sentence. Although my husband was sitting next to me, I still felt terrified and alone. I took a deep breath, and I fought back the tears that were building up within me.

Then, within seconds, he said other words that were so comforting, that they softened the first, and I will never forget them: *"We're in this together."* It's been a couple of years, and he has kept this promise.

Throughout my life, I've heard a lot of words that fell into the category of *bad news*, but this bad news was terrifying. I knew that it was going to be a gigantic mountain to climb.

In 2006, I was diagnosed with chronic kidney disease. Since then, I've had this anticipatory fear hovering over me like a dark, gray cloud, that felt like an unwelcome companion. As my kidney function gradually declined, I began to realize that it wasn't a matter of *if* I would need dialysis, but *when*.

On the drive home, I looked at Kenny and said, "Well, this stinks."

He nodded. "Yeah, it does. But, you can do this. Like you always say, take it a day at a time." (I hate it when he reminds me of my own words.)

He continued, "Look at all of crap that you've gone through in your life. You can do this. You've got this!"

It didn't feel that way. I felt like I was just hit with a bucket of ice water, and I couldn't see even a tiny glimmer of light beneath this new blanket of darkness, which quickly engulfed me.

Dialysis is such a loaded word. Essentially, it means that my kidneys can't keep me alive anymore without a machine. In a way, it's similar to life support, only you get to go home. This news shook my world, and brought me face-to-face with my mortality. Suddenly, the sense that I had control over my life began to crumble to dust. I was angry and terrified at the same time. And so, this new challenge – this new journey – began. Was I ready? No! But that never stopped adversity from finding me. I thought, ready or not, here comes another storm! I had to brace myself.

As I walked into the hemodialysis treatment room for the first time, I was reminded of an experience I had when I was five years old, when I was brought to kindergarten. I had that same feeling of terror — the sense that I was going to be left with people I didn't know, who were supposed to take care of me. In this situation, these people were going to be responsible for keeping me alive. *Damn*, I thought! *That's frightening!*

The dialysis center is a gigantic room, with light green painted walls containing huge posters with inspirational messages. There are two nursing stations in the middle of the room. Lining the walls are 20 patient recliners, all tan in color. There's a computer and a small TV set on one side of each chair.

The ominous dialysis machine, which is nearly five feet tall, is on the other side.

The dialysis journey begins...

During each treatment, the blood pressure cup is affixed to my left arm, automatically registering my blood pressure every 30 minutes. If I'm having more frequent drops in blood pressure, then the machine registers every 15 minutes. You have no idea how annoying this can be if you haven't experienced it.

Two gigantic, 15 gauge needles are inserted into my right arm, which houses my access site — the graft. (Some patients have a fistula.) I've gotten used to the fact that insertion of these two needles will hurt for a few seconds. After the needles are put in place, I can't move this arm, or the dialysis machine will flash a red light, and beep.

Bee-beep. Bee-beep, Bee-beep... All day long, someone's machine is beeping to indicate a problem with blood pressure, pulse, or venal pressure. At the end of treatment, there's a different sound: *Beep-beep (pause) Beep-beep (pause) Beep-beep.* It's a sound that I look forward to, because it means that my treatment is finished, and I can go home soon.

Physically, it's uncomfortable to sit in an hard dialysis chair for three hours. I have chronic lower back pain, which is aggravated by sitting in this position, and I use a neck pillow to alleviate some of the neck discomfort. Often, I shiver because my blood is being cooled, to prevent my blood pressure from dropping. My blanket helps minimally. Sometimes my fingers get numb. Sometimes I get a headache, or I'm nauseated. At times, three hours feels like an eternity. Let's just say it's not a pleasant walk in the park.

At times, I glance around the room, and I wonder what other patients are thinking and feeling. Do any of them feel like scared little kids too? Are they frustrated? Angry? Sad?

Afraid? At one time or another, I've felt all of the above – sometimes in rapid succession. It helps to divert my attention. Thank God for iPads and televisions. But still, it's hard to ignore the continuous *Bee-beep, Bee-beep, Bee-beep*.

When the dialysis machine isn't beeping, the blood pressure cuff is inflating every 30 minutes! Again, it's so annoying! Since I do a lot of writing on my iPad, I must stop mid–sentence, when I feel it inflating. If I don't, it keeps retaking my blood pressure until I comply. It feels as if the blood pressure cuff sometimes has a life of its own, and can be quite temperamental.

Including travel time, I spend nearly 12 hours a week in dialysis-related activity. This isn't exactly how I envisioned spending my retirement years, but I recognize that there are probably worst places that I could be. This thought brings me some comfort.

Over the last couple of years that I've been going to dialysis, I have grown to care about and respect the staff. It helps to chat with them, and make the best of the situation that I find myself in. They're friendly, compassionate people, and they work hard. They rarely sit down, and are always busy either interacting with patients, or doing other tasks. They know every patient's name, and are upbeat and personable. This has helped me to feel comfortable and cared for.

I also spend time doing the footwork required to get on and remain on transplant lists. I've met with transplant teams from several hospitals, and had multiple tests. This can be frustrating and stressful, especially knowing the average waiting list is 5 to 7 years. Sometimes I wonder if I'll live long enough to actually receive a donor kidney. Then, I need to remind myself to stay in the *now*.

Being on dialysis is a rough journey. There are some days when the sadness grips me, and it's difficult to shake off the sorrow that I feel. Sometimes I want to cry, because I feel completely powerless over my circumstances. Other times, I'm angry, because I feel that my body has betrayed me.

I feel fatigue most of the time. Yet, regardless of how I might feel, three times a week, I still have to get dressed and go to the dialysis center. It doesn't matter if the sun is shining, or if it's raining or snowing. In some ways, it feels like a part-time job, or a prison sentence, depending upon my mood on that particular day.

Physically, I must deal with the discomfort of large needles. Sometimes I get bruises if the nurse or technician is having difficulties when inserting these needles. When I'm not feeling well, the staff members often remind me that while I'm sitting in a chair doing nothing, my body is doing a lot of work.

When I come home from dialysis, to enter my house, I must walk up four steps, and then another six steps. Often, by the time I walk in the door, I can barely catch my breath. I feel as if I've run a marathon. As soon as I open the door, I walk to the bedroom and plop on the bed. That's how tired I feel.

I have to limit foods with potassium and phosphorus. If I eat foods high in phosphorus, I get itchy. However, the most difficult dietary change is a 32-ounce maximum daily fluid allowance. I never realized how uncomfortable it feels to be thirsty.

Prior to dialysis, I never thought about being thirsty. I simply quenched my thirst without a second thought. Now I must limit my fluid intake, because my ability to urinate has decreased significantly, and some day, it might be gone completely. That means that the only way to remove bodily fluid is through the dialysis process. There are times when the physical discomfort of thirst has been so overwhelming, that I go to sleep early, so I could avoid it.

Periodically, a clot forms in my access graft, due to blood pressure plunges. Then dialysis can't be performed. When this happens, I see a doctor who specializes in clearing this type of clot. It's a complicated procedure, done with local anesthesia, and requires sutures. Sometimes it can take a couple of hours. Since I have frequent blood pressure plunges, I must have this procedure done every few months. Not fun!

All things considered, I recognize that I've grown over the past few years. I'm not the same terrified person who walked into that building for the first time. At the onset of this new journey, I was so overwhelmed, that I struggled to summon even a morsel of inner strength. Now, most of the time, I accept my circumstances.

In writing this chapter, I've revisited some of the trauma related to my kindergarten experiences. In significant ways, I believe that this current journey has helped the little 5 year old within, who was terrified of kindergarten, being left in an unknown and possibly dangerous place. I felt these same feelings when I first walked into the dialysis unit. Working through this experience has indirectly healed some of those lingering emotional wounds from the past.

My kindergarten experiences left me with emotional scars; fears of being deserted, and then the fears of unanticipated bodily harm. In getting past similar fears related to the dialysis center, I've now come full circle, and I've conquered this old wound on a different level. I recognize that I can and have survived.

A few weeks ago, I has an accident in dialysis, which necessitated adding an update to this chapter. When this happened, it was traumatic. Now that a few weeks have passed, I've bounced back, and can even find some humor in the situation, and I'm grateful, because my injuries could have been much worse. So, let's just call this update *fifty shades of purple.*

The last time I had a black-eye and facial bruises, I was 5 years old, and they were caused by my mother. (See Chapter 7 – Kindergarten.) A few weeks ago, at the end of my dialysis treatment, I incurred my second set of facial bruises.

Since dialysis normally causes low blood pressure, sitting and standing blood pressures are taken at the end of each treatment. Because I have orthostatic hypotension, when I stand up, my blood pressure plummets, but I usually experience warning signs, like dizziness, lightheadedness, or hot flashes. But not this time! I had no forewarning. One minute, I was standing and talking to the nurse, and the next minute, I was laying on the floor. I was told that I fainted.

When I first regained consciousness, my surroundings appeared blurry and dark, as if I was in a dimly lit room. I felt disoriented. Within seconds, the room gradually became lighter. Then I heard a voice that sounded as if it was far off in the distance.

"Nella, Nella, are you OK?"

Although I felt dazed and confused, I was trying to get off the floor, and I recall that the nurse, Emily, helped me into the chair. I remember feeling weird, as if was drugged or under the influence.

Then Emily told me that I had a big goose egg on my forehead, and she called for an ambulance, because she felt that I needed to go to the E.R. to be examined to rule out a concussion, and to possibly have a brain scan. Although I was dazed, I was impressed by how quickly the staff sprung into action to help me.

About 10 minutes later, an ambulance arrived, and two EMT's brought me to the E.R. While there, I was examined, and a brain scan showed that there was no bleeding on the brain, so I was discharged and instructed to use ice packs.

Initially, the pain was incredibly intense. With each passing day, the pain is decreasing. As I write this chapter, nearly 2 weeks later, my right eye, forehead and cheek are still sporting what I call fifty shades of purple, with some areas turning blue, green and yellow. The goose egg is gradually decreasing.

(As a side note, my doctor has now prescribed medication to raise my blood pressure, which should prevent this from happening again.)

I keep reminding myself of a cliché my wise father-in-law would often say, "This too shall pass." It's just not passing fast enough for my impatient soul. While, my husband, who is the eternal optimist, continues to remind me that it could've been worse. If I had fallen forward rather than sideways, I could have broken my nose and my teeth. Okay, I guess I should be grateful.

So, as I reflect upon this situation, I have come to a few conclusions. My Higher Power was looking out for me, and I'm not an easy person to kill!

Chapter 29
To Be, or Not to Be

⁓

I'M NOT A BIG SHAKESPEARE FAN, but I was always interested in the play, *Hamlet*. Prince Hamlet, the main character, was a deep thinker and an intense guy, who was struggling with grief, depression, and anger. He addresses philosophical questions that I too have struggled with, in this famous quote:

"To be or not to be, that is the question. Whether 'tis nobler in the mind to suffer the slings and arrows of outrageous fortune, or to take arms against a sea of troubles, and, by opposing, end them."

In modern language, these heartfelt musings might sound something like this: Is it better to be alive or dead? Is it nobler to put up with all of the horrible things that life tosses in our direction, (and accept that we're just helpless victims), or to stand strong and fight against all those troubles, and rise and overcome them? (Not give up.)

From time to time, I've thought about this quote when I was faced with yet another challenge, or, as Hamlet would call it, "the slings and arrows of outrageous fortune." And although I've briefly pondered if life was worth living, I've never seriously considered the alternative. Since, in the past, I never felt that my life had been physically threatened, I never really thought about death.

However, I think it's impossible to be diagnosed with a life-threatening illness, and not think about your own mortality – the possibility that you might die a lot sooner than you might have expected, or sooner than you would have preferred.

Suddenly, I had to face the reality that I had an expiration date – I wasn't immortal.

The truth is that I was feeling sick, and I knew my kidneys were gradually failing. Although I tried my best to retreat into denial, my symptoms were increasing. I was constantly nauseated and vomiting, and I lost my appetite. Loss of appetite was a big warning sign, because this has never happened to me before. Even though I felt miserable, I just didn't want to think about it.

The wording of my diagnosis upset me the most – "end-stage renal disease." I hated these words! They sounded so final and hopeless. They implied that my life might be ending soon, and this scared the hell out of me! When you reach *end-stage*, there's nowhere else to go.

My doctor explained that I could live a long time on dialysis, and eventually hope for the possibility of receiving a kidney transplant. However, I still couldn't get past the wording of this diagnosis – *end-stage renal disease*.

Before I was diagnosed with end-stage renal disease, I never seriously pondered the fact that eventually I was going to die. I think most people put this reality in the back of their minds. It's just too frightening. Whenever the thought presented itself, I pushed it away. However, after being hit with a large bucket of ice water — of being told that I needed dialysis in order to stay alive — my thoughts were all over the place.

In the days and weeks following my diagnosis and proposed treatment plan, I began to seriously obsess about my own mortality. In doing so, the above quote from Hamlet returned to the front of my mind. However, I didn't think about this newest challenge in isolation. I thought about it in conjunction with all of the other pain, struggles, and challenges in my life, and all the adversity that I thus far have endured, some of which I have still not healed from.

My first thought was, "God, c'mon, can you give me a break?" Then I thought to myself, "Dialysis? Do I want to go through this shit?" This question was rhetorical, because the answer was obvious. Who in their right mind would want to go through this?

I knew that I had the inner strength, and resilience. However, I didn't know if I had the physical energy to fight this battle. I was tired and weary. This diagnosis also affected me emotionally. It put me face-to-face with powerlessness concerning my life, and it triggered grief.

I was also dealing with a lot of other stressful and energy-draining medical issues. I have fibromyalgia, degenerative disc disease, and osteoarthritis. Most of these illnesses translate into chronic daily pain, from the moment I open my eyes, to the moment I go to sleep at night. However, they aren't life-threatening.

Once again, I thought about Hamlet's question: is it better to live or to die? Did I want to live, or, did I want to throw in the towel?

The problem was this: I'm a fighter. I'm a survivor. I don't have the mental mindset that seriously includes giving up as an option. The words: *Fuck it, I give up*, are not a part of my vocabulary. In my mind, giving up would be allowing the disease to win, and I have never conceded or walked away from a fight in my life.

So the answer was clear. Since giving up was not in my DNA, my only option, regardless of how I felt, was to "take arms against the sea of troubles."

Weary or not. Tired or not. Fed up or not. Pissed off or not. Terrified or not... my choice would inevitably be to fight. As I've said, I never walked away from a fight, and this was no different.

Chapter 30
A Sense of Humor

M Y SENSE OF HUMOR HAS SAVED my sanity more times than I can remember. The ability to laugh has helped me to stay strong and cope with the rough patches, especially during the last few years of my life. It's also helpful that my husband has a great sense of humor, and can help me to laugh when I'm feeling downhearted. A sense of humor can be heart-healing. And then, there's my nephrologist, who's charming and witty, and can bring a smile to the face of even the crankiest patient. I'm so happy that he has a sense of humor, too.

My neurologist's father was on dialysis, and some of his other family members have kidney disease, so he understands this disease on a personal level. Also, like myself, he agrees that it's important to have a positive attitude, and laughter is sometimes the best medicine.

The other day, I told him, "This isn't exactly where I expected to spend my retirement years."

Drawing upon his own sense of humor, he replied, "Well, you rubbed the lamp, and I'm Aladdin. I'm the genie that popped out.

Then I responded, "Well, in that case, I want another lamp and a different genie. And, by the way, this wasn't one of my wishes."

We both had a good laugh. You've got to laugh. It's healing, it's good for the soul, and it's better than crying. It's amazing how healing that laughter can be, and how it has distracted me when I was feeling depressed or upset. My sense of humor has helped me survive the worst of circumstances over and over again.

One day, despite of all the discomfort that I was feeling, in an effort to find some humor in my situation, I wrote this poem:

The Dialysis Blues
*How does one find serenity
in the dialysis center?*

*Re-focusing thoughts
is a pretty good start.
Sitting in a chair,
Six feet apart.*

*Two hours have passed,
one hour to go.
I'm freezing my butt off,
like I'm sitting in snow.*

*The dialysis machine,
So fierce and yet meek,
is helping me get through
another great week.*

*So, let's just pretend
we're all at the beach,
though frankly, that's quite
one hell of a reach!*

*My butt's getting tired
From sitting in the chair.
Dialysis is helping,
But my butt doesn't care.*

*The room's filled with warriors.
They sit wall to wall.
And the nurses are awesome.*

They give it their all.

Now, forty-five minutes
are left on the clocks.
But I'm still freaking cold.
Wish I wore heavier socks.

I can't wait to go home.
I'm as hungry as hell.
Just thirty-five minutes,
And the machine rings the bell!

Chapter 31
Timeless Moments and Words

REGARDLESS OF HOW MUCH TIME PASSES, there are some moments and words that I will never forget. They have been so powerfully etched in time, that they have transcended years. They live in the realm of timelessness.

Some have brought joy to my heart, while others have brought tears to my eyes. Every moment has words and a story, and every smile, and every tear, also have their own tales to tell. Some words were so comforting to me that they felt like a warm, gentle hug, while others were so painful, that it felt as if I was being slashed with a sharp razor blade.

I still remember the extraordinary moments in my life: the happiness I felt when my husband asked me to marry him, the unsurpassed moments of joy on my wedding day, the moments of excitement I felt when I performed in a band, the feelings of accomplishment when I graduated from college and graduate school, the thrill I experienced when I typed my name in Amazon, and saw my first book. And, of course, the in-between moments that marked the ebbs and flows of my life.

In contrast, there have also been tragic moments and words – particularly, the damages incurred by abuse, the death of loved ones, and the heavy burden of making decisions concerning someone else's life, and the pain of hearing heartbreaking words from people I once cared about. In hindsight, I think that perhaps these dark, timeless moments too had their purpose. In their own way, they have contributed to my personal and spiritual growth.

The absence of words isn't often talked about, but this void can be equally powerful. Sometimes I think about the words I should have said, and instead, remained silent. The unsaid words will always haunt me the most. Then, there's the silent treatment I've experienced from Stella. There is violence in intentional silence. It is a powerful form of abuse.

As mentioned elsewhere in this book, challenges and adversity aren't new to me. Throughout my life, I've heard a lot of words with strong sentiments attached to them. In fact, it seems like my life has been one challenge after another, with no breathing room in between. Each challenge has felt like a monumental mountain to climb.

Often, what appears to be the worst challenge is simply the most recent one, because this is the one which currently preoccupies my thoughts. Therefore, from my perspective, it seems to be the worst one. However, if I browse through all of the difficult challenges I've experienced throughout my life, there are a few that stand out as the worst, because of the deep, unhealed wounds that I've incurred.

Every time a new challenge, a swerve in direction, or a new frightening dilemma presents itself, I always wonder if I'll have the strength to handle it. And yet, I've consistently received help from God, and the support and encouragement of my husband and my therapist, who have reminded me of how much strength I have.

Often, my husband has more faith in me than I have in myself. He's right; I always seem to handle the obstacles that life places in my path. Nevertheless, there are times when I'm frustrated, and I ask God: Can you give me a break? A reprieve? When I change my perspective, it helps. This begins by refusing to define myself solely by my troubles, and refusing to allow them to be the center of my life.

Perspective is reality. Words are powerful. Words matter!

Chapter 32
Forgiveness Revisited

I N THE EPILOGUE OF MY SECOND BOOK, *The Forgiveness Journey Workbook,* I wrote these words:

"Life always seems to challenge us, and push us to grow on deeper levels, even if we're not particularly thrilled to walk the forgiveness path yet again. However, each new opportunity to forgive, affords us the gift of additional wisdom and insight. Each of us will walk many forgiveness journeys throughout our lives. It's unavoidable."

After writing two books on the topic of forgiveness, I find myself revisiting this topic once again, for a few reasons.

First, after writing this memoir, I became aware of unhealed wounds. I discovered that, although I've been able to release much of the resentment concerning my tragic childhood, I've been unable to let go of the anguish of being disinherited, and, at this moment, I'm not sure if I can ever heal from and let go of this wound.

Second, a few weeks after I began dialysis, and after my first book was published, my sister created a firestorm which led to our permanent estrangement. This situation left me with another new resentment, and I was again reminded of how difficult it can be to forgive family members. (See the Chapter *Sisters* for further details.)

Concerning her reactions to my book, even though Stella knew the contents prior to publication, she was still disturbed when my book was published. Instead of speaking to me directly, and having an adult conversation, she ignored me, and encouraged her adult children and her sister-in law to confront me and argue with me.

This firestorm became worse because she learned that her son, Jim, my 35-year-old, married nephew, read my book, and even sent me a complimentary text. When my sister discovered this, she became enraged. My nephew then texted me: "My mom went ballistic. She's upset with me because your cousin told her I read your book. She's screaming and crying. She's hysterical!"

I understood that he was upset, but I couldn't understand why she "went ballistic" simply because he read my book, especially since he's isn't a child, he's a married adult with children. Anyhow, I'm guessing that he was further pressured, because eventually he stopped speaking to me and blocked me on Facebook. Nonetheless, I don't have a grudge toward Jim, because he wasn't rude to me, unlike his, sister, who berated and threatened me. He just ran away, like a frightened little boy.

This was the second time his sister Molly used Facebook to be disrespectful and hurtful. The first time this happened, she was angry because I refused to co-sign her loan, so she publicly posted a Facebook status telling everyone that I was adopted, so I wasn't her *real aunt*, writing: "You were never blood anyway. Now I don't consider you family." Although there wasn't an apology for this first offense, I forgave her, because I was sure that her mother instigated the situation.

I believe that her reaction to her mother's hysteria concerning my book, led her to write me a private text, where she reprimanded and threatened me. And so, as I reflect upon my niece's repeated attacks, I recall how difficult it can be to forgive someone who is vicious and unapologetic. I'm not quite there yet. In fact, right now, I'm not sure if I can ever forgive her and let go of the resentment that I feel.

Sometimes I think about the all of the times when my niece

called me, and asked me to visit her mother, who needed support, and I put aside whatever I was doing, and did so without a second thought. And so, part of the work I need to do now is to learn to accept that just because I choose to help someone, doesn't mean that I can except a certain outcome, and blame people when I feel unappreciated.

When I speak at public events, I'm often asked the question, "Is everything forgivable?" In the past, my response has been, "Yes. I believe so." I explain that we forgive for *our own* well-being. When we do so, we often experience some relief. Therefore, our well-being and healing are the main focus, rather than the specific offense. However, as I write this chapter, I'm re-evaluating some of my previous beliefs, as I explore new insights based upon new experiences.

Now, I'm looking at forgiveness from a broader perspective and a different level of awareness. I'm seeing that the forgiveness process isn't an all-or-nothing affair. It's more like the tides in the ocean, moving forward, ebbing and retreating, and then inching forward again. Perhaps, sometimes we forgive on different levels, or in increments.

Little did I know that I would be called upon to revisit formidable forgiveness opportunities so quickly, and, in the process, I'm learning how hard it can be to follow my own advice. Once again, I'm keenly reminded of how difficult it can be to scrub my heart of the pain and disappointment that I've incurred from these new offenses, as well as the ongoing pain I still feel.

As a result of new experiences, insights, and a different perspective, here are some of the questions regarding forgiveness that I'm revisiting:

How many times should we forgive someone who repeats offenses, and remains unapologetic?

Why is it more difficult to forgive people who are still alive, rather than those who are deceased?

And finally, the most important question of all: How do we forgive and let go, and maintain the state of *letting go* long-term?

I don't know all of the answers yet. However, I plan to continue to work toward forgiveness for my *own* healing and well-being. It's interesting to note that these new experiences have brought me back to where I ended my second book:

"The forgiveness journey never really ends. Just when we think that we've mastered the art of forgiveness, another unexpected situation will confront us and challenge us to forgive yet again. We are consistently reminded that forgiving isn't as easy as we might have remembered. It takes work, and sometimes it can be a formidable task."

Chapter 33
Doom-isms & Goodbyes

Y HUSBAND KENNY AND I have completely different personalities. He doesn't worry about the future. He doesn't contemplate *what-ifs*. He often says, "If I can't change something, or do anything about it, I'm not going to worry about it." For the most part, he lives by this credo.

If you have an emergency, you would definitely want Kenny to be with you. He has the ability to stay calm, and focus on solutions, even in the worst of circumstances. He is methodical, and gives off a calming, confident energy, that will help to relax anyone who is panic stricken. (More than once, I've been that person.)

Give Kenny a guitar, a TV set, or a funny YouTube video, and he's perfectly content. He's always in the moment, and he doesn't need to work hard to find joy. In contrast, I have to struggle to maintain joyfulness, to stay in the present moment, and to avoid worrying and envisioning doomsday scenarios about the future. I practice mindfulness and meditation every single day, while my husband seems to be innately mindful.

My husband hasn't had insomnia a day in his life. He just closes his eyes and falls asleep, sometimes within seconds. On the other hand, I need to use a machine that plays the relaxing sounds of ocean waves, or I would *never* fall asleep. Even then, sometimes I toss and turn all night long.

I think that his temperament and worldview was greatly influenced by his childhood experiences. Kenny takes after his father, who was also easygoing. His dad didn't worry, and he also projected a calm presence. In fact, his father's favorite saying was, "This too shall pass."

Kenny's parents always complimented, encouraged, and supported him. They were warm, loving people, who were not histrionic or crisis-focused. They didn't look for reasons to create drama. They didn't get angry about nonsense. In contrast, my family never met a tragedy they didn't like. If there wasn't a tragedy, then they were more than happy to create one.

I grew with what I call doom-isms, which reflected my mother's negative philosophy of doom and gloom. She regarded these adages as valuable pearls of wisdom. However, they were all based upon fear and negativity. Here were a few of her favorites:

1. Laugh today, cry tomorrow
2. Tragedy comes in threes
3. We live in hope and die in despair
4. When it rains, it pours.

Laugh today, cry tomorrow

Whenever my sister and I laughed, my mother would evoke the cautionary adage, "Laugh today, cry tomorrow." The omen implied that you had to be careful if you were too happy, because you were bringing misery upon yourself, without even realizing it. Too much laughter was guaranteed to bring about tears.

Tragedy comes in threes

This adage usually applies to death. If one person dies, then two more people will die, because death *comes in threes*. But this also applies to other tragedies, especially airplane crashes.

We live in hope and die in despair

Life is difficult. We keep hoping for better things, that will never happen. And so, we will eventually die in despair, because life is hopeless and none of our dreams will be realized.

When it rains, it pours

If something horrible happens, it's guaranteed that worse things are going to happen again and again.

————

Through therapy, I have recognized how this mindset has influenced every aspect of my life, and I did a lot of work to shed the remnants of trauma-drama. First, I had to acknowledge that I was unknowingly repeating some of these learned patterns. I would automatically panic when I didn't know how to handle certain situations. I never learned coping skills. When anything unplanned happened, I imagined that the outcome would be catastrophic.

I worked hard to learn how to stay calm in the midst of crisis, and look for solutions or ways to cope. Over the years I've gotten much better at trying not to panic when I've encountered upsetting situations, and learned to be still, and maintain serenity in the midst of chaos.

My relationships with my parents ended because of their physical deaths, although not without dangling loose ends. My relationship with my sister ended because the toxicity became too overwhelming. I'm reminded of Dr. Maya Angelou's cautionary advice, "When people show you who they are, believe them the first time." I didn't do this.

I believe that everything happens for a reason. Sometimes we hate the reason. Other times, we don't understand the reason.

Sometimes it takes a long time and a lot of hindsight reflection to comprehend the reason, and most of the time, we just dwell within the realm of loose ends and unanswered questions. Hey, that's life!

I have learned that one of the most important truths in life is this: if I don't learn the lesson, it will keep repeating itself in different situations, with different people, and with increased intensity, until I pay attention and finally *get it*.

There is one lesson I struggled to learn, because I didn't want to. That's knowing when it is time to walk away from a relationship. *Goodbye* was the lesson I needed to learn. It was the solution, but I resisted, because goodbyes have always been difficult for me.

The word *goodbye* has had different meanings during different periods in my life, and for different relationships. There were times when saying goodbye was liberating and healing. In a different context, saying goodbye was frightening, painful, and sad. Sometimes it's been a combination of conflicting feelings.

There have been many journeys throughout my life that included goodbyes, sometimes by choice and sometimes due to circumstances beyond my control. However, with every goodbye, I've learned something new. If nothing else, I was given an opportunity to recognize my inner strength, and the ability to move forward. Eventually all the tears have subsided. We can't cry forever, because we have to get on with the business of living.

In the poem *After a While*, Veronica Shoffstall, beautifully articulates her journey from a frightened little girl to an empowered woman. In this evolving story of personal growth, she explores triumphs over challenges, the gradual development of inner strength, accrued insights, the pain of losses, and the struggles, the fears, and sadness that we might experience each time we must say goodbye.

She closes her poem with these words: *"You learn that you really can endure, that you really are strong, and you really do have worth. And you learn, and you learn. With every goodbye, you learn."*

Chapter 34
Closing Doors

FTER NEARLY THREE DECADES of working with my therapist, she's retiring. In terms of this relationship, it is an end of an era. Although we plan to stay in touch with one another, I realize that the nature of the relationship is going to change significantly. We will not be speaking every week at a particular time, as we've done for nearly three decades.

I feel despondent. In fact, I'm saddened beyond words, and lately, the sorrow I feel has been expressing itself primarily in the form of tears, anxiety and nightmares. If you've read this book, then you know I have had abandonment issues and nightmares my entire life, so I guess it makes sense that this explosive change would trigger these feelings.

There is an adage that says, "When one door closes, another door opens." Although an important door in my life is quickly closing, the other door has not yet opened. So, there's a gap. This gap feels dismal, and terrifying. Even when and if this new door opens, it will not erase the sadness I feel that as this current door is closing. A relationship with a new therapist cannot compete with, or replace the relationship I had with Dr. H. for nearly three decades. Besides this, it is anxiety provoking just to think that I need to start again with someone else. I'm frustrated.

Roughly speaking, over the course of 29 years, I've had around 1500 sessions with her. That's a big number! Yet, if you ask me to remember what I said in each of these sessions, I couldn't tell you that answer. I only recall snippets. However, I can say that I am a significantly different woman today than when I first met her, and she has greatly contributed to this change.

As this door begins to close, I find myself tearing up, as I reflect upon this relationship, what is it has meant to me, and how it has greatly contributed to my life journey. My therapist has supported and accompanied me, as I relived, and attempted to heal from past childhood trauma and abuse, as she's helped me to address current traumas and adversity.

Aside from my husband, she has supported me through the shock I felt when I learned that I was adopted, the sadness I felt when my mother died, the pain I experienced when I was disinherited, the terror I felt when I learned that I needed to be on dialysis, and the sorrow I felt when my sister created an unnecessary firestorm in my life, a few weeks after I began dialysis. Throughout the years, she has also assisted me in navigating through mood disorders. In fact, she was always there, even during times when it might've been uncomfortable and trying to do so.

I remember when I first met Dr. Hoffman. She has short dark brown hair, she wore glasses, and she had a nice smile. I also recall that she had a sense of humor, and I liked that about her. In fact, it's interesting that I immediately liked her. This was unusual for me, because it usually takes me a long time to trust, and to warm up to people.

At that time, I was in emotional turmoil. I had been in recovery for five years, and I was dealing with the fallout of child abuse, incest, PTSD, flashbacks, and a mood disorder, without relying upon alcohol to help me to escape my feelings and pain.

Dr. H. (as I refer to her,) has always been caring, compassionate, honest, supportive and understanding. At times, although she might not have agreed with me, and confronted me, she never judged, me or made me feel bad about myself.

Although I've always addressed her by her surname, over the years, I've come to see her as a family member that I've never had, but have always wish for; someone who was always there, despite some struggles that we've occasionally had with one another. To be honest, at the beginning of our relationship, sometimes I wasn't the easiest person to get along with. There were times when she could have easily exited our relationship, but she chose not to do so.

I don't believe I would've achieved this level of personal growth without the relationship that I've had with her. She has become an important part of my history, and, in many ways, my legacy. And so, I plan to stay in touch with her. I just cannot imagine my life without her in it. Still, I know that our relationship will change, and, quite frankly, I don't like change and the uncertainty that comes along with it.

In my chapter entitled *Doomisms & Goodbyes*, I briefly talk about how difficult goodbyes can be for me. Although this isn't a goodbye, in some ways, it feels this way. It's a goodbye to the type of relationship we've had, and that's enormous. This change also requires new and creative ways to approach this relationship now. At the beginning, this is going to feel... well... awkward. There will be new rules and boundaries, and I don't really quite understand them yet.

So, as I say goodbye to Dr. H. as a therapist, I will say *hello* to our new relationship, and I'm happy that she wants to keep me in her life too.

Chapter 35
Lessons Learned

"Hope is that thing inside us that insists, despite all evidence to the contrary, that something better awaits us if we have the courage to reach for it, and to work for it, and to fight for it." (Barack Obama)

THIS QUOTE HAS ALWAYS spoken to me, and it still does. Amid adversity and ongoing challenges, I've always had hope and resilience, even if it was just a smidgeon. Within *"all evidence to the contrary,"* I still had *"the courage to reach for it, work for it, and fight for it."* Sometimes hope was the only thing that kept me going, as I daydreamed about better days to come.

Winston Churchill famously said: "If you're going through hell, keep going." I'm guessing he meant that you shouldn't stop for coffee. Rather, you should move as quickly as possible, and get the hell away from dangerous and frightening situations.

During my childhood, I wasn't able to do that. There was nowhere to go.

However, I've also experienced other challenges and adversity which didn't provide an exit door. And so, I had to cling to hope, and pray for resilience, even when I was feeling consumed and engulfed by a dark blanket of despair.

Writing this book has led me through a different kind of hell. At times, I had to slowly walk through a trail of memories, re-living and re-examining the most upsetting parts of my life, while trying to make sense of these experiences, and identify the growth, the healing, and the possible learning lessons they could offer me.

In *The Divine Comedy*, Dante Alighieri keenly observes, "The path to paradise begins in hell." It appears that, like others, I too had to go through hell to find a piece of paradise. And, like Churchill suggested, if possible, it's a good idea to move quickly and "keep going."

To summarize, I've lived through these major crises:

- Physical assault
- Verbal and psychological abuse
- Sexual molestation
- Struggles with mood issues, especially anxiety and depression
- Alcohol abuse issues
- Family estrangement
- Grief, loss & depression
- Chronic medical issues
- Life-threatening health issues, leading to dialysis

My life has been... well, let's just say – eventful. Yet, here I am – I'm still standing. When I think about the person I was decades ago, it feels as if I'm looking at someone else. Sometimes I think to myself, *Who was that person, and where did she go?*

I can see that I have gradually evolved from a frightened, guarded child, to a more empowered, courageous, and confident woman. I'm happy about that. At the same time, I'm annoyed that it took so long. And...honestly... I'm not yet where I would like to be.

Without a doubt, I know that I would have never been able to move forward on this difficult life journey, facing one challenge after another, especially life-threatening medical issues, if I didn't have the love, understanding and support of my husband, and the help and guidance of my therapist.

I've faced and walked through various painful challenges. I've learned how live with disappointment, to expect the unexpected, accept the unacceptable, and to acknowledge that life is filled with loose ends and unanswered questions. If I didn't have hope, I wouldn't have survived.

There were so many times when I felt as if I were going to drown – and yet, I didn't. Instead, I clung to the waves of each storm, afraid, yet with unyielding determination, and I survived. Although, not without scars. Still, often I've surprised myself.

Although I don't remember every moment of my life, I do remember the most significant moments that have changed it. Most of them are included in this memoir. There were times when I wished that I could forget some of the most painful moments, but that would also have prevented me from remembering the noteworthy, joyful moments, and I wouldn't want that.

As I see it, when life throws stones at me, I have two choices. Either I could see those stones as weapons, and allow them to assault and defeat me, or I could collect them and build a strong house. I could choose to use them to my advantage, or allow them to cause my demise. When I was younger, there were many times when I allowed them to defeat me. As I've gotten older, and learned from different experiences, I've tried to gather these stones to build a formidable fortress.

When I've viewed my challenges and struggles simply as disasters, I felt like a helpless victim, and have tumbled into the dark, bottomless pit of depression. In contrast, when I was able to change my perspective, and used my experiences to help someone else, then growth ensued.

Courage is as important as perspective and hope. Sometimes, it was only in hindsight that I was able to recognize moments of courage. For example, during my first surgery for the peritoneal dialysis catheter, right before being taken into the operating room, I suddenly burst into tears. I knew that my life was going to drastically change, and I was terrified.

Several months later, when I had my second access surgery for the hemodialysis catheter and graft, I didn't have the same reaction. Something had changed, and that *something* was *me*. Although the circumstances in my life were actually more stressful, the braver me was able to handle them more courageously, and with a greater sense of serenity and acceptance.

Author and activist Elizabeth Cady Stanton wrote: "The moment we begin to fear the opinions of others, and hesitate to tell the truth that is in us, and are silent when we should speak, the divine floods of light and life no longer flow into our souls."

It took decades before I was able to accept the fact that some people might not like me. When I was younger, disapproval upset me. It was so important to be liked. Sometimes I would twist myself into a people-pleaser just to gain approval. Then I'd get angry with myself. As I've gotten older, I've become less concerned with the opinions of others. I've learned that it doesn't matter if someone dislikes me; it's not a reflection of who I am as a person.

Regarding perspective and insights, Holocaust survivor, Dr. Viktor Frankl, wrote a book entitled: *Man's Search for Meaning*, where he shares important observations. His words have helped me to re-define the circumstances of my life, and make attempts to search for the insights and learning opportunities from my past experiences. Frankl talks about what he calls "the last of the human freedoms":

- Even though our freedom or our possessions can be taken from us, no one can take away our freedom to choose our attitude.

- When we are powerless to change our external circumstances, we are forced to focus inward, and change ourselves. This includes our perception of our situation.
- In the midst of pain and adversity, we can still find our meaning and purpose in life. Moreover, doing so can greatly influence our healing.

It's interesting how changing my perspective regarding kidney failure has motivated me in different ways. Before I was diagnosed with end stage renal failure, I never thought about the concept of time, or how long I would live. However, this diagnosis made me acutely aware of the reality that I have an expiration date. I'm not going to live forever. Ouch!

I used to be a procrastinator and easily bored. I would begin a project with elated enthusiasm, and then lose interest, and fail to complete projects that I started. However, now I'm more action-driven, and self-disciplined. I complete all of my projects. What changed? My new diagnosis was a wake-up call which changed my perspective.

I've always struggled with mood issues, primarily anxiety and depression. In my experience, emotional pain is far more devastating than physical pain. Physical pain usually subsides or ends. Emotional pain can linger indefinitely, and be unrelenting. Adding PTSD or panic attacks into the mix can be terrifying and immobilizing.

The weight of some of my life challenges and adversity has often pulled me into the darkness of depression. In this state, it's difficult to find hope. And yet, each time I've found myself in this place, I grabbed onto the tiny glimmer of hope, and the light got brighter, and eventually escorted me out of the darkness.

Over the years, I've learned that, when I feel depressed, I

must force myself to take actions, even when my depression fights me every step of the way. This includes getting out of bed, taking a shower, getting dressed, getting out of the house, and getting out of my own head. Self-pity is absolutely the worst choice, because it increases depression.

Although life has often left me battle worn, despite bouts of depression, I've always been resilient. I have endured and bounced back. Sometimes I've learned from my mistakes. Other times, I had to repeat them to understand the learning lesson. For some reason, and I'm not sure exactly why, regardless of the adversity, giving up was never a serious option for me. Although, at times temporarily immobilized, eventually, I've always been able to to walk through each obstacle I've encountered, even if that meant that sometimes I had to *crawl* rather than walk.

In addition to walking through obstacles, I've also encountered bridges. Bridges are meant to take us from one place to another. Ideally, they're supposed to take us from where we are to where we want to be. Sometimes my chosen bridges have led me to dangerous places, so, I had to burn bridges to get away from toxic people, and this fire lit my way to move forward in my life.

Although I physically removed myself from toxic situations, guiding my mind away from the associated memories required additional and ongoing work, which I've achieved through mindfulness exercises.

I used to spend a lot of time ruminating over the past, and worrying about the future. *Living in the now* is an important concept that I've learned in 12-step recovery groups, which is really a form of mindfulness.

When I began dialysis, my first thought was, "OMG, do I have to do this the rest of my life?!" I was terrified.

Then I learned about the possibility of receiving a donor kidney. I had to do a lot of footwork to be evaluated for each donor list. Now, I'm on a couple of donor recipient lists, but the waiting time is five to seven years. That feels like a long time. Going to dialysis three days a week makes the waiting time feel like an eternity.

Sometimes I wonder if I will ever receive a kidney. *What if... I don't?* Recovery groups call this "stinking thinking," because this negative train of thought will not take you anywhere helpful. When my mind goes to this place, I use the thought-stopping technique that I talk about in my other books. I say to myself: "Stop! Change thought! Redirect thinking!" It helps.

In reality, no one can predict what will happen tomorrow. Life circumstances can change in a heartbeat. How many healthy people could have predicted that they would die from Covid-19? Life is unpredictable, and the *one day at a time* philosophy has helped me through many moments in my life.

As I work hard on practicing meditation, mindfulness, and living in the now, I try to tell myself that, if it's meant to be, I will receive a kidney. If not, I will deal with life on dialysis. Ultimately, I believe that I won't leave the physical realm and transition to the afterlife, one moment before, or one moment after, I am supposed to, according to God's plan.

Mindfulness is closely linked to perspective. Some of the adversity which I've encountered has, at times, crumbled the ground beneath my feet. I can still remember that frightening feeling. I had to face the reality that the only thing that I *did* have control over was how I chose to perceive and respond to my circumstances – perspective. Then it was important to avoid defining myself solely in terms of the adversity that I was facing.

Another aspect of perspective involves looking at the entire picture. If I never experienced a cloudy, chilly, stormy day, then I wouldn't be grateful for the warmth of a sunny, summer day. As Dante implies, if I never walked through hell, I would never have found a piece of heaven. I wouldn't have fully appreciated the precious moments of love, quiet serenity, and elating emotions like joy, happiness, gratitude, and accomplishment.

Of course, I wish that I never dwelled within the pitch-black darkness of sorrow, or experienced the emotionally painful upheavals of physical assault, sexual violence, verbal and emotional abuse, and losses.

I wish I didn't have to spend my retirement years at a dialysis center, hoping that I'll get a transplant, and being forced to follow a renal diet, with water restrictions that result in the intense discomfort of thirst. I wish I didn't feel itchy, or nauseated. I wish I didn't have headaches, physical discomforts, anxiety, depression, chronic fatigue, and all of the other shit that I have to go through on nearly a daily basis.

I wish I didn't have to return from dialysis so fatigued and weak, that I can barely walk up a few stairs, because I can't catch my breath. But I can either accept it or get pissed off about it, and the latter isn't going to be helpful.

And still, I believe that the God of my understanding has not deserted me. He never guaranteed that I wouldn't have struggles. I believe that He has given me the strength and resilience to get through every single struggle in my life.

It goes without saying that I wish my life wasn't bombarded with one challenge after another. But it is what it is. Shit happens! This might sound weird, but it could always be worse, and I am grateful for the blessings in my life, and for the lessons I've learned and shared with others. Despite all the challenges, I'm most grateful for my husband and the special, loving relationship that we have shared over the decades.

Walt Whitman said, *"Do I contradict myself? Very well then, I contradict myself, (I am large, I contain multitudes.)"* I can identify with this. At the same time, I wonder if I'm really contradicting myself. I think it's more about evolving and becoming different versions of who I was yesterday — last year —20 years ago.

One thing is for sure, the challenges in my life have changed me. As a result of each challenge, I have emerged a different person. Although, at times, I've been wounded, I have always emerged a stronger and more enlightened woman. Sometimes it took a while before I was able to understand the right lesson. However, regardless of the circumstances, lessons were always learned.

I've faced and walked through various painful challenges. I've learned how live with disappointment, to expect the unexpected, accept the unacceptable, and to acknowledge that life is filled with loose ends and unanswered questions. If I didn't have hope, I wouldn't have survived.

There were so many times when I felt as if I were going to drown – and yet, I didn't. Instead, I clung to the waves of each storm, afraid, yet with unyielding determination, and I survived. Although, not without scars. Still, often I've surprised myself.

Chapter 36
Advice to my Younger Self

W HEN I THINK ABOUT WHAT ADVICE I would give to my younger self, it would need to be divided into a few categories. What could I possibly tell the little girl trapped in frightening cycles of abuse? At the same time, I recognize that the little girl was a strong kid. She had faith and hope. She was resilient. She hung in there.

Since I was impulsive during my younger adult years, I would encourage this version of me to avoid making emotionally charged decisions, without considering consequences. I would also try to offer comforting advice specific to particular life-changing events that I found myself in. Finally, I would suggest some helpful tips that I've learned from life experiences.

I would begin with advice that could have prevented poor decisions, and avoidable, self-defeating mistakes. As I reflect upon this category, I can see a common thread. Often these mistakes were based upon anger or fear, where I didn't look at, or care about, the possible consequences, until after the fact. Some poor decisions and behaviors were based upon unhealed past wounds.

For example, unconsciously, I would attempt to change the outcome of situations that were similar to prior traumatizing events . This is called the *repetition compulsion*, which is defined as repeating past unresolved situations, hoping that, this time, we will achieve the desired outcome that we didn't get the first time. Often, for me these scenarios involved female authority figures that reminded me of the toxic relationship that I had with my mother.

Other impulsive, unhealthy behavior involved using and abusing alcohol and comfort food, to escape reality and emotional pain. Eventually, some of these behaviors led me to 12-step recovery groups. Ultimately, my experiences in 12–step recovery groups were the best thing that ever happened to me.

Regarding advice specific to major life-changing events, it can get complicated. Would I have listened? I don't know. For example, what advice would I have given to myself when I was 39 years old, and I was shocked to learn that I was adopted? I wonder if there were any insights or any advice that I could've said to my younger self that would've offered some comfort.

My mother died when I was 43 years old. What advice could I have given my younger self to ease the pain of this loss? Would my last conversation with my mother have been different, if my older self told the younger Nella that this would be the last time that my mother and I would speak on the phone? I'm not sure how I would've handled this, if I had this information.

What if I told my younger self that she was going to be disinherited? Knowing this, would I have had the courage to confront my mother about this? Is there any advice that would have helped the younger me? I'm fairly sure that, if I knew this information, I would have confronted her. I wouldn't been able to visit her for those four years, and celebrated the holidays with her, without addressing this.

What if I knew ahead of time that my sister and her adult children would eventually treat me in the same cruel and toxic manner as my mother did? Also, would I still have reconciled with my sister, knowing that she was going to pick up where my mother left off, and treat me like a scapegoat? I'm fairly sure that the answer is "no."

I've had kidney disease for over ten years, before it progressed to the point where I needed dialysis. Were there any words that could have prepared me for the inevitable? What could I have told myself that might have eased the pain and the fear of being on dialysis?

All of the questions related to life changing events are complicated. What-ifs don't have definitive answers. However, there's some general advice that isn't related to major turning points in my life, that I still wish I had known. This advice is based upon insights and life experiences. Here's this type of advice I would share with my younger self:

Never Give Up

This is the most important advice that I can give you, younger self. Regardless of what happens in your life, even if it seems like you're in a pit of darkness that will never end, do not, I repeat, do not give up. Everything passes, if you just ride the wave. Heed the words of writer and poet, Maya Angelou:

"Just like moons and like suns, with the certainty of tides, just like hopes springing high, still I rise."

Savor and Appreciate Every Moment

I would tell my younger self to pay attention! You can't recapture this moment again. The older you get, the faster time seems to pass, and you will begin to recognize the importance of each moment of your life. When I look back on my life, I say to myself, where did the time go, how did it pass by so quickly? How many moments did I waste by worrying about tomorrow or ruminating about yesterday? How many beautiful sunrises and sunsets did I miss?

Animal Companions

Consider adopting an animal companion. My animals have been my greatest spiritual teachers, and they have all brought much joy to my heart. I've learned so much from each animal that I've had the pleasure of knowing. They've taught me to live in and enjoy the present moment, and strive toward loving without conditions. In some cases, my animals have also reflected back to me some of my flaws that I needed to look at, and work on.

There's something about the joy of seeing a wagging tail and an expression of appreciation, that cannot be replaced. This is despite the fact that my happiest *hello* has always been my saddest *goodbye*, because I have outlived my pets. And yet, knowing this still wouldn't stop me from adopting and rescuing. I can't even imagine the emptiness I would feel if I didn't have an animal in my life.

Be Grateful

Appreciate what you have, and those who love you. Don't wait until people are gone to realize how much they've meant to you. The clock cannot be reversed. Also, there is always something to be grateful for. Sometimes it's basic: a roof over your head, food in your refrigerator, love in your life, the ability to open your eyes every morning, and being given the opportunity to experience another day.

The Objects of Your Desire

My foxhound Alex loves food more than life itself. He will do anything to get even a little morsel of any type of edible item. (And sometimes, the item isn't edible, like a napkin. I'm sure that it smells like a piece of food to him.)

There have been times when Alex could have gotten injured just trying to find a little piece of food. He was so laser-focused on getting the object of his desire, that his game plan became unimportant.

Although it's funny, I remember times when I've attempted to get something desired, and avoided looking at the potential obstacles in the way. In doing so, this has often backfired. And so, my advice would simply be: look at all aspects of the situation, including consequences, before you jump. You might be jumping off a cliff.

Respect, and Toxic Relationships

There are a few valuable insights that I've learned regarding respect. First, respect should be earned, and it needs to be mutual. If you're being disrespected, then you have no obligation to respect that person back. Further, enforce your boundaries, and refuse to allow anyone to disrespect or abuse you emotionally or physically.

As I've re-examined the unhealthy relationships that I had with my mother and my sister, I've realized that the longer I remained in these relationships, the more difficult it was to leave them. If you find yourself in a toxic relationship, run quickly to the nearest exit.

Control

You can't control or change anyone but yourself, and that requires a lot of work and time. People will only change because they want to, not because you're trying to force them into doing so.

Trust Your Inner Wisdom

Maya Angelou has keenly observed that, *"You might not remember what people said or did, but you will always remember how they made you feel."* If you feel uncomfortable or distressed when you're in the presence of a particular person, you need to look at that, and figure out why. Trust your instincts. Your inner wisdom is speaking to you.

Materialism

Never allow money or material possessions, to be your God. The most valuable things in life cannot be bought, and don't have a dollar value.

Worship

Never fall into the trap of worshipping another human being.

Balance and Patience

Laugh more, worry less. Strive toward having more patience. Anything of value takes time.

Anger & Resentments

Although I've written two books concerning forgiveness, and letting go of resentments, I recognize that sometimes forgiveness can be difficult, and might even feel impossible. Sometimes it can take a long time. This is especially true if the offender is still alive and unrepentant We forgive others for *our own* well-being, sometimes in increments, and it doesn't always include reconciliation. This process takes time, and is sometimes a forward and backward dance. (See chapter: *Forgiveness Revisited*)

Life is a Patient Boomerang

If you live long enough, you might notice that life is a patient boomerang. Even if we're not there to see it happen, the wrong-doings of others will eventually catch up to them, just as our wrongdoings will catch up to us. The Judeo-Christian Bible says that we reap what we sow. The Hindus and Buddhists refer to this boomerang as karma. The law of attraction asserts that we attract the same energy that we emit into the world.

Yesterday and Tomorrow

Younger self, try to avoid obsessing about yesterday, or worrying about tomorrow. The past only has the power that we choose to give it. Don't waste too much time obsessing about things that couldn't be changed. Instead, try to identify the learning lessons. If you feel that you need to heal from past experiences, don't be afraid to do the work.

We don't know what the future will bring. Usually, while we're worrying about one thing, often we're blindsided by the unexpected. Try to avoid rehearsing doomsday scenarios that will probably never happen. Put your energy to better use.

Autocorrect

Try to learn from your mistakes. Good judgment comes from experience. Experience usually comes from bad judgment and stupid mistakes.

Find Joy

Play, laugh, find joy in the simple things, and have fun. A sense of humor can get you through a lot of tough spots. Don't be too serious. Discover what makes your life worth living. Never stop learning. Don't live your life to make other people happy.

This past summer I found great joy in planting roses and watching them grow. You can't put a price tag on that. Don't be the person that says, "I'll be happy when..." Happiness is only found in the present – in the journey, rather than the destination.

Faith

I talk about faith and God is another chapter. For purposes here, it helps me to pray to the God of my understanding. I'm not religious. I'm spiritual. But I believe, without a doubt, that God helps me, and gives me strength and insight. If I didn't believe in God, I would never have been able to tackle and overcome all of the stresses and challenges that I've experienced in my life. I also believe in an afterlife, and that I will see those I love on the other side someday. I believe that my love ones are with me right now in spirit form, and they guide me and help me in different ways. Consider exploring your spiritual self.

Heartache, and Being the Light

Poet Amanda Gorman beautifully writes: *"For there is always light, if only we are brave enough to see it. If only we're brave enough to be it."* You can learn from everything that happens in your life, even upsetting circumstances. Look for the light in the darkest of moments. As Gorman asserts, *"there is always light."*

Finally, as Jack Kornfield asserts:

"In the end, just three things matter:

How well we have lived

How well we have loved

How well we have learned to let go"

Chapter 37
Lessons from the Yellow Brick Road

"You've always had the power, my dear.
You just had to find it for yourself."
(Glinda, the Good Witch of the North)

THE FIRST TIME I SAW THE MOVIE, *The Wizard of Oz,* I was a child. Since then, I've watched it every year during the holiday season. In fact, Glinda's words have helped me many times throughout my life, whenever I needed to find the power, resilience, and strength within me.

When I was a child, I've often daydreamed about a tornado whisking me away, and catapulting me to a place where I felt safe and loved. I even preferred the Wicked Witch of the West, to my mother, who I feared, and perceived as the Wicked Witch of the Bronx. I saw Dorothy's witch as less terrifying.

Over the years, each time I've watched the movie, I've gathered new insights and life lessons, depending upon what was going on in my life at the time. There were so many times when I've felt exactly like Dorothy: helpless and terrified. Like her, I didn't realize that my answer has always been right under my nose, and within my grasp.

I particularly identified with Dorothy's feeling of being lost, and not knowing where to go, and what to do next. It's a terrifying place to be. At the same time, I also identified with, and applauded her courage, determination, and strength. In the face of adversity, she never gave up, and continued to find ways to get what she needed. She never lost her focus.

Dorothy was resilient. She overcame each obstacle, and continued to follow the yellow brick road. I've also been blessed with resilience. I guess you could say that I've followed my own *yellow brick road*, and, like Dorothy, I continued to bounce back, and overcome the obstacles that blocked the path ahead.

I'll have more to say about Dorothy and her journey at the end of this chapter. For now, however, I want to speak about her traveling companions, and identity some similarities that I share with each of them.

The Scarecrow

The Scarecrow and I shared the mistaken belief that we lacked intelligence. A long time ago, he was ridiculed, told that he was stupid, and he never stopped believing this. Was he as brainless as he perceived himself to be? Absolutely not! In fact, he was the problem-solver in many of the situations that Dorothy's group encountered, and was possibly the smartest one in the group.

When the trees became angry, and told Dorothy and her friends to stop picking their apples, (in the land of Oz, trees are personified), the Scarecrow outsmarted them by telling them that their apples had worms, and he and his friends didn't want them anyhow. This infuriated the trees, who started to throw their apples at the group, thus allowing them to pick up the apples and eat them. That doesn't sound stupid, does it? Sadly it didn't matter. In the face of all evidence to the contrary, the Scarecrow still perceived himself as stupid.

The Scarecrow's problem began when he gave way too much credence and importance to someone else's opinion of him. He internalized it, believed it without question, and allowed it to control his life, his self-image, and how he felt about himself.

Been there – done that.

After needing to repeat the fifth grade, no one would have been able to convince me that I wasn't stupid. Every time I saw my former classmates, I felt as if they judged me as stupid, because I was left back. My low self-esteem was reinforced by the fact that my parents treated me as if I was worthless and a burden.

In fact, as mentioned elsewhere, I continued to believe this for a long time, until I was in my 30's. I returned to college, and maintained a 3.9 grade point average. It was only then that I could see, much to my own surprise, that I am intelligent.

The Tin Man

The Tin Man (aka Tin Woodsman) felt that he lacked, and needed a heart. The movie is based upon the Oz book series authored by L. Frank Baum, where the Tin Man's story is explained in greater detail. To summarize, when the Tin Woodsman was put back together, after being hacked apart by the Wicked Witch of the East, his body was replaced with metal parts. However, they forgot to give him a heart. He thought that, because he didn't have a physical heart, he would be unable to feel emotions, especially love.

Was the Tin Man really heartless? No! Actually, he was sensitive and kindhearted – quite a warm and sweet guy! He felt Dorothy's pain, and empathized with her. That shows compassion. However, he just couldn't recognize this.

As I was working on this chapter, and explored this particular character, I began to think about what it actually means to be heartless. It's such an embarrassing character flaw. No one wants to be seen as heartless or cold-hearted.

Despite this, there have been many times in my life when I

wished I could be heartless and insensitive. It would've saved me a lot of pain. Then again, being heartless would mean that I wouldn't be able to experience happy and joyful moments. That's not a sacrifice I'd be willing to make.

I have a few more musings concerning the heart, so bear with me. There are two aspects to the heart. First, we have a physical heart, a body organ, which has nothing to do with emotions. However, it's vitally important, because it beats and keeps us alive.

Second, we have an abstract reference concerning the heart, when we're talking about our emotions. I'm not sure how and when this came about, but somewhere along the line, we equated the heart organ with our feelings.

The Tin Man didn't need a physical heart to experience the feelings that we attached to our hearts. He was kind, warm, and lovable, and, as the saying goes, "he wore his heart on his sleeve." Nonetheless, like the Scarecrow, his perception prevented him from seeing this.

The Cowardly Lion

The Cowardly Lion was such a lovable, adorable character. At first glance, he seemed to be afraid of his own shadow. It's hilarious! When his tail touched him, he tried to run away from it, terrified, because he felt that it was stalking him. The symbolism seems funny, but this is exactly what fear does. I hate to admit how many times I've scared myself so much, with little evidence of real danger, that, in no time, symbolically, I too was trying to run away from my own tail.

The Cowardly Lion was also overly dramatic and intense, because he didn't know how to handle his anxiety, or calmly find solutions. (With his histrionic personality, he would've fit in perfectly into my family.) He was also ashamed, and felt like a failure, because he believed that he lacked courage. However, in reality, his perspective simply prevented him from seeing his own courage. He didn't understand that courage isn't the absence of fear, it's forging ahead in spite of fear.

Like the Lion, I too have struggled with seeing my own courage. When I share my story in meetings, or at speaking engagements, people often tell me that, given the challenges in my life, I was rather courageous. And yet, I've always found it difficult to recognize it. I've gotten much better at this.

Final Thoughts on Dorothy's Journey

Dorothy went on a long journey, and had to overcome many obstacles, because she believed that she didn't have the tools and skills she needed to solve her problem. And so, she was seeking solutions outside of herself. This journey could've been avoided if she simply looked within to begin with.

Like Dorothy, there was a time when I too felt like I had to find solutions outside of myself. It never occurred to me that I would be able to look within to access my inner strength and find answers. I only saw myself as the problem, rather than the solution, so the last place I thought that I would find answers was within.

The most notable example of this happened over three decades ago, when my life was gradually crumbling around me. I was experiencing a lot of the emotional pain, and the consequences of unaddressed and unhealed childhood abuse. I was overwhelmed, and inundated by flashbacks, and other symptoms of PTSD. I just wanted to find relief, and something that would make this pain stop – at least temporarily. Unfortunately,

It took a while before I could find my solution.

There comes a time when you must realize that searching for solutions from others may not provide you with the answers you seek. For Dorothy, it was that moment when she pulled back the curtain, and saw that the wizard was just a person. He wasn't the "all powerful wizard." He was not the solution, and he didn't have the power to help her.

When this reality hit her, she was shocked, disappointed, and angry. I remember these feelings, thinking, *Oh shit! What do I do now?* I know these words weren't in the movie, but I'll bet Dorothy was thinking this.

My defining moment was when I realized that my go-to solutions weren't going to solve my problems, or get rid of my pain. They were just temporary pseudo-solutions, and they created a host of other problems. And then suddenly, that glass of wine or comfort food, lost their magic, and simultaneously, lost their power to control me, because I was able to see that they weren't helping me.

Like Dorothy, I had to realize, the hard way, that the external solutions were not really problem solvers. Initially, this revelation was accompanied by feelings of anger, disappointment, and fear. Eventually, they morphed into enlightenment.

Dorothy's life actually became more unmanageable, because she was putting herself in dangerous situations. However, she couldn't see this. Until Dorothy was able to see that only she had the power to solve her issues, and nothing outside of her could do so, she was stuck.

This brings me back to Glinda's words at the beginning of this chapter. The power is always within, even when it doesn't feel that way. Throughout this memoir, you've read about a lot of adversity and challenges that I've experienced. I think anyone would agree that some of them seem like horrible stories.

However, if you look beneath the specific circumstances, you might notice that there are underlying and consistent themes: inner strength, resilience, hope, and faith. I think that these qualities all fall into the category that Glinda defines as "the power within you."

There were many times in my life when I didn't realize that I had the power within. Still, like Dorothy, I just kept putting one foot in front of the other, and hoped that eventually, as Churchill said, I would walk through and past hell.

Epilogue

UTHOR HARUKI MURAKAMI ELOQUENTLY writes: *"And once the storm is over, you won't remember how you made it through, how you managed to survive. You won't even be sure whether the storm is really over. But one thing is certain. When you come out of the storm, you won't be the same person who walked in. That's what this storm's all about."* As I complete this memoir, I can strongly identify with these words.

It was difficult, painful, and, at times, overwhelming to write this book. I didn't realize how upsetting it would be, until I began writing. I had to dig deep within me, probing the darkest crevices of my mind, and documenting some of my most painful memories, experiences, and emotions. However, I strongly felt that my story needed to be written and shared.

Upon completion, I felt so much relief, as if a heavy burden has been lifted from me. I've also experienced some healing and letting go. At the same time, I recognize that there are just some experiences that I will never fully get over, and I've come to accept that complete healing is impossible. I've also learned to live with certain limitations, and function in spite of them. I believe that these limitations do not, in any way, diminish me as a person.

As I wrote this memoir, I was able to gain more clarity, and recognize that, throughout my life, and through each challenge, every obstacle, every *storm*, and each chunk of adversity, I had strength, resilience, and a lot of guts! For some unknown reason, I still do. I'm a survivor! It is my hope that if you're able to identify with any of my experiences, you'll see that you can transcend your adversity, and eventually identify yourself as a survivor too.

Aside from other challenges, recovering from a toxic family, and the aftermath, has been a long, arduous, and tiring journey. Sometimes, when I look back over the years, I think that I have shed way too many tears over people who probably weren't worthy of a single teardrop. At the same time, every teardrop offered me a learning opportunity, as well as insight, healing, and cleansing relief. Further, each shedded tear has helped me to expunge some of the toxicity that I absorbed when I was around my toxic family members.

Life will always have challenges, but, as the singer/song-writer and cancer survivor, Nightbirde, says, *"You can't wait until life isn't hard anymore, before you decide to be happy."* Exactly right!

My journey has led me to exactly where I need to be at this moment in my life. Each challenge, every heartbreak, every tear, every joyful moment has molded me into the woman I am today. From a philosophical perspective, everything can be seen as a learning lesson, especially the difficult experiences.

That doesn't mean that I'm overjoyed by the traumas and challenges I've experienced. There have been many moments when I looked to the heavens and said, *Hey God, why me?* or *C'mon, give me a freaking break!* From a broader perspective, I believe that I am, and we all are, ongoing encyclopedias of life lessons. These lessons only have value if they're shared to help someone else.

I have worked hard to make sure that my past did not dictate my future. As Viktor Frankl says, even in the worst of circum-stances, we have the freedom to choose our perspective and our responses. I will never understand why my life has had so many challenges, and so, to achieve serenity, I've learned to live with the unanswered questions.

This might sound strange, but despite all of the challenges

I've experienced, I've learned valuable lessons, gained wisdom, had a pretty good life, and, most of the time, in recent years, I'm happy. I've learned that it helps a lot to have acceptance, flexibility, faith, and a sense of humor. My challenges have helped me to gather strength, grow, and gain deep insights.

Yes, I have a few scars, and I'm still in the midst of serious health challenges that are incredibly stressful and anxiety-provoking. However, I've risen above much adversity, and have fulfilled many of my dreams. I went back to college and graduate school. I worked as a counselor. I performed in bands. I enjoy painting, and have even sold some of my artwork. I have just completed this 3rd book, and my other books have helped a lot of people.

I've also been married to the same man for over four decades, we have a great life together, and I love him just as much today, as I did the day that I married him. I still laugh at his jokes. How many people can say that?

I grew up in a toxic atmosphere. Aside from the abuse, everything – I mean, everything was a tragedy, and doomsday was imminent. There was constant drama, and I was always holding my breath, waiting for the next crisis. If someone had a cold, my family thought they might have pneumonia. If someone was too thin, my family suspected that they might have cancer. If it was raining, then, like Noah, my family was ready to collect wood, and build an ark.

Although I'm not biologically connected to my family, my childhood history and experiences were far more powerful than my DNA, and I, too, had this tendency to gravitate toward drama. I had to do a lot of hard work to overcome this crisis mentality.

I've made great strides to evolve over the years. I am not the same woman I was 5 years ago, 10 years ago, and certainly, not

20 years ago. I think that if the different versions of me were to meet each other, they would probably meet as strangers. They might not recognize one another. Maybe they wouldn't even like each other.

Now, I try to live my best life, one day at a time. I get through challenges, sometimes one minute at a time, and I try to enjoy each moment. I have learned to pay attention! When I was younger, I missed a lot of beauty around me, because I failed do so. I was focused on the past, or worrying about the future. Wasted time and energy! Little by little, I'm evolving into the woman I want to be.

More importantly, when it begins to drizzle, I no longer have an urge to collect wood, and build an ark. Instead, I'm learning how to dance in the rain!

www.ingramcontent.com/pod-product-compliance
Lightning Source LLC
Chambersburg PA
CBHW030240030426
42336CB00009B/185